fear falls away

# *f*ear falls away

*and other essays
from hard and rocky places*

by Janice Emily Bowers

The University of Arizona Press   Tucson

The University of Arizona Press

© 1997 Janice Emily Bowers

⊗ This book is printed on acid–free, archival–quality paper.
Manufactured in the United States of America

02 01 00 99 98 97 6 5 4 3 2 1

Library of Congress Cataloging–in–Publication Data

Bowers, Janice Emily.
Fear falls away and other essays from hard and rocky places /
Janice Emily Bowers.
p. cm.
Includes bibliographical references (p ).
ISBN 0–8165–1717–7 (cloth : alk. paper).–ISBN 0–8165–1718–5
(pbk. : alk. paper)
1. Santa Catalina Mountains–Description and travel.
2. Mountains–Arizona–Description and travel. 3. Natural history–
Arizona–Santa Catalina Mountains. 4. Bowers, Janice Emily.
I. Title.
F817.S28B68 1997
917.91'0943 – dc21                                                         97–4659
                                                                              CIP

British Library Cataloguing–in–Publication Data
A catalogue record for this book is available from the British Library.

For Steve, the best of companions

# contents

# acknowledgments

Grateful acknowledgment is made to the editors of the publications in which the following chapters were first published: "Still Hunting" appeared as "Hospital Flat, Pinaleño Mountains" in *South Dakota Review*, and "A Broken Mountaintop" appeared as "Mount Graham, Pinaleño Mountains " in *North American Review*.

Thanks to the friends and family who have enriched my life, and to everyone I have mentioned by name in this book: Steve McLaughlin, Betsy Pierson, Renée Rondeau, Gordon Rodda, Laurie Wirt, Kirk Vincent, Richard Felger, Ray Turner, Jeanne Turner, Doug Elliott, Tony Burgess, Paul Young, John Baade, Cathy O'Dea, Phil Urry, Heather Urry, Barbara Kingsolver, and Tom Wise. Thanks especially to Tim Schaffner, Steve McLaughlin, Jennifer Shopland, Joanne O'Hare, and Pat Shelton for reading various versions of the manuscript and helping to give it shape and sense.

# 1

## remembering mountains

These are the mountains I know best, the Santa Catalinas. I must have a thousand images of them in my mind, overlaying one another like double negatives redoubled many times. Every time I see them, which is nearly every day, another image forms, and when I close my eyes, my vision of them is a picture palimpsest. For instance, seen from the center of town, the westernmost ridge is a flat, outsize zigzag pasted on the sky. But seen from the west, this ridge gains another dimension. It expands and unfolds like a magical paper flower dropped into a glass of water. Cliffs jump out. Vegetation obscures sight lines. The ridge itself is not, it turns out, a knife edge; it is an arm and shoulder reaching down to embrace a canyon previously hidden from view. Other disparate pictures mingle in my mind's eye, too. Somehow, each image retains its own integrity. Though merely part of the whole, it demands to be regarded as the sole and simple truth.

Yet what do I know about the truth of these mountains, when, after glancing at them at least once a day for seven thousand consecutive days, I still cannot picture their skyline in its entirety. I start at the west, as always, and imagine Pusch Peak, a lopsided triangle, rising toward Pusch Ridge, a sloping line drawn by a shaky hand. Then Table Mountain, a hard and angular surface, then the gap-toothed protrusion known as Prominent Point, and beside it the slender spire of Finger Rock, then Mount Kimball's small, blue peak, but what's next? These are supposedly the mountains I know best. It's a peculiar kind of knowledge that won't resolve itself into repeatable pictures or chartable images or graphable data. Evidently, glancing is not the same as seeing, and noticing is far from remembering.

All the mountains around here are like that. Not easy to remember, not even—or not necessarily—easy to love. My friend Maureen hates them. Their flatness, as if painted onto the sky, strikes her as unforgivably banal; and their arid, rocky slopes remind her of all she's lost in moving to the desert from a more reasonable climate. Someone who knew only the Sierra Nevada of California and its snow-flecked scarps, paternoster lakes, and jagged, pyramidal peaks would find it hard to imagine, much less understand, the mountains of southeastern Arizona. To describe them, I must first enumerate everything they lack. We have little running water and few springs. Even at high elevations, we have no land above 12,000 feet, therefore no permanent snow, no timberline, no krummholz, no alpine zone, no pikas or marmots, no cushion plants of negligible size and enormous age. We had no glaciers, therefore possess no cirques, no arêtes, no hanging valleys, no moraines.

Our mountains are not the stuff of posters and coffee-table books. They are rather the stuff of wary beauty and abiding love, a beauty that lies as much in the contrast of rock and leaf as in splendid views, a love that lies less in easy responses than in intimate acquaintance, doggedly pursued.

I grew up with mountains. Yes, not *in* mountains, but *with* them, far enough away that they seemed separate from my immediate surroundings, close enough that everything I did happened in their shadow. This was in Upland, a medium-sized town in southern California, a town like those around it with orange groves, vineyards, parks, and clapboard houses. Wherever you went in town, whether to the old post office on the railroad tracks or to the Carnegie Library on D Street, you could lift your eyes—"lift them unto the hills," as the Bible said—and you would see the San Gabriel Mountains, a line of big, blue, steep-shouldered peaks. The peaks overlapped slightly along their edges like members of a wedding party who must all be fitted into the same photograph. Later I discovered that drawings of mountains gained infinitely in verisimilitude by the simple device of showing them as slightly overlapping lines, and I followed this formula even though the ambiguity bothered me: which peak was forward, which one back, and where did this one end and that one begin? It would be many years before I learned to fit appearance to reality, the truth that adjacent peaks share a projecting ridge, that the overlapping lines represent canyons invisible from a head-on view, that mountains seen from afar are not the same as mountains seen up close.

All these years later, I still know the names of only three peaks in the San Gabriel Mountains: Ontario and Cucamonga Peaks, twin guardians like a pair of stone lions on library steps, and peeking out from behind them, the bare rock dome of Mount San Antonio, inevitably known locally as Mount Baldy. I remember wanting to know the names of the others, but my parents couldn't tell me. We were like indigenous peoples who name only the useful plants in the local flora. Having no use for peaks as such, we didn't need to know their names.

Today I have no idea whether these mountains are beautiful. Certainly I thought so as a child, but to children all mountains, like all mothers, are necessarily beautiful. Walking to school with them every day, I came to know their lineaments as well as the faces of my own family. My mountains were lined and worried looking, like my mother's face. Their color, somewhere between gray and blue, was a steely, chilly shade like my Great-uncle Jay's eyes. Pines and firs made a serrated line along the crest, tiny triangles, each representing a single tree, or so I understood it. When I tried to count them, though, I always lost track. Those were massive and solid peaks. They reminded me of my father's five sisters, unfashionably plump yet reassuringly huggable women. Later, when I learned of mountain peaks called The Sisters, the name made perfect sense to me. Miraculously, my mountains occupied no space at all, or no more space than a window blind, and when my mother explained that Mount Baldy looked smaller than the other peaks only because it was farther away, I couldn't quite believe it. The mountains seemed most beautiful in the winter, when snow filled in the wrinkles. But they were beautiful in summer, too, if more ordinary, and I felt guilty about having a preference. Didn't my parents love my sister and me with equal fervor?

If we had moved to Upland as exiles from, say, the flatlands of Kansas or the swamps and hammocks of Florida, I wouldn't require mountains as I do. But we didn't. Born within sight of mountains, I was imprinted at birth. No matter where you are in Upland, my mother taught me, the mountains are north. This was a fact as important as my address. If you knew that the mountains were north, you would never get absolutely lost. You can put the mountains on your right hand or your left, my mother said. You can face them or turn away, yet always they remain north from our house. It seemed miraculous, a solid, unchanging fact to set against much that seemed ambiguous. Thus mountains were built into my internal gyroscope. Without them I am adrift.

What strikes me these days when I visit my hometown is how big those mountains are. They admit no horizon to the north; the mountains themselves are the only horizon, and the world of shopping centers, housing developments, and freeways on their far side is something you must take on faith. More often than not, you must take the mountains themselves on faith, since at times you can't see them either. Some days you can't see through the filthy air to the end of your street, much less to the mountains fifteen miles away, and as objects recede into the distance—street lamps, traffic lights, palm trees, apartment buildings—they lose their natural colors. The middle distance becomes a film shot in black and white. Standing in the driveway of my sister's house, I look to the north—to the mountains—in vain. Only X-ray vision could penetrate that smoggy curtain. The mountains are there, for I can feel their presence, the way I am aware of my husband beside me, even when I am asleep. They struggle to breathe, to see, to hear through their envelope of smog. They are dying. And always I think the same thoughts: what if I had never known these mountains at all; and why, when I had the chance, didn't I trouble to know them better?

To know what you have while you still have it, that's the thing, I say to myself as I drive north through the summer-green San Rafael Valley, the Huachuca Mountains on the one hand, the Patagonia Mountains on the other. The road rises and falls with the rolling landscape, flinging hilltop against sky, then dropping it down. On the banks of the road, delicate sprays of grasses are momentarily picked out against the blue, then smeared against the general green.

This is the classic southeastern Arizona landscape—the summer garden of grasses, the flat, blue mountains encircling the horizon, and the white and gray clouds piled over grassland and mountain alike. Beautiful, unspoiled country, or it would be if not for cattle and occasional ranch houses. The deleterious effects of grazing are not so apparent at the height of summer; at least, and in any case, grazing is better than suburban sprawl, garish ranchettes, mobile home estates—the innumerable forms of development that have despoiled southern California in the three decades since I was a child.

I keep remembering the once-empty landscapes of my childhood and how they are now buried under asphalt and concrete and steel, and how I didn't know what I had until it was gone. And I wonder if the same fate awaits this evocative landscape, if in fifteen or twenty years, it too will be dead. Or, if it remains untouched, whether I will be here to see it.

What bothers me most is that I might not be here. My husband, Steve, who teaches at the university, will be up for tenure next year, which is almost, but not quite, the same as being up for promotion. If he gets tenure, it is the same. If he doesn't, if tenure is denied, he is fired and has to leave the university within a year.

It's a peculiar system that has little but tradition to recommend it. You must prepare a tenure package, a kind of elaborate résumé that lists all your publications and research projects, explains your philosophy of teaching, and generally toots your own horn as loudly and persistently as possible. As part of the package, a number of experts in your field must write letters of recommendation for you. You submit the package to the promotion and tenure committee in your department, which recommends for or against tenure, then passes your package on to a higher committee that makes its own recommendation, then turns over the package to a third committee, where the final decision is made. The process takes an entire academic year from start to finish.

In Steve's department, you must submit your tenure package during your sixth year at the university. You can, if you want, apply for tenure sooner than that, which is what Steve did last year at the recommendation of his department head. He expected to sail right through—and indeed his department and his college forwarded his package with enthusiastic recommendations for tenure—but the committee at the highest level voted against it. A few weeks later he opened an envelope to find a form letter that began, "I regret to inform you, but . . ." No reason was given for denying tenure.

Because his *was* an early submission, he was allowed to stay in his job another two years. We should consider ourselves fortunate. Outside academia you don't usually get a second chance, nor, when you are fired, do you have a year's grace period in which to find a new job. That's what Steve has been doing this past year—applying for positions at other universities in the event that he is again turned down for tenure.

Now that I might be moving away from Tucson and its mountains, I have been driving city streets with eyes burned raw by nostalgia for what I could lose. Always I have noticed how, minutes before a summer thunderstorm, the smell of dampened earth permeates the nostrils, and that after rains, the pungent odor of creosote bush wafts in from the surrounding desert. But I failed to appreciate the silky indigo skies as summer days metamorphosed into night, nor did I think to treasure the play of light on the Tucson Mountains. At such moments I cannot imagine a life apart from this particular landscape, these particular mountains. My instinct is to make certain that I really see them now, while I have the chance. In another year, they might be remembered mountains. I must make sure that I have something to remember.

Three years ago I drove for the first time through the wheat-farming country of central Montana, a landscape striped with pale blonde wheat and gray–black earth, an endless swatch of corduroy. In that country of limitless horizons, field met sky in a continuous, undulating line. Some people love it, I hear. I found it oppressive. Never before had I understood how badly I need limits to my horizons.

Where I live, open country ends at the mountains. From all around the horizon they beckon—the peaks I know, the ones I don't, the shadowed canyons hidden by their own slopes, the distinctive ridgetop silhouettes like rumpled bedclothes or wrinkled skin. In this corner of Arizona, there are roughly two dozen named mountain ranges, depending on what you call a mountain and where you draw your boundaries. Their names, listed on a page, could be mistaken for a poem, a gentle, lilting music, like water swirling around a stone basin or walking–sticks tapping on a bedrock slab: the Santa Catalinas, the Santa Ritas, the Patagonias, the Rincons. Some, based on Indian names, are difficult to pronounce at first. Chiricahua, Huachuca, Baboquivari. Say "Cheery–caw–wah," the guidebooks advise; say "Wah–choo–caw." When I first saw the word Baboquivari in print, my throat and tongue balked. No sounds came out of my mouth at all. Eventually, someone taught me to say it like this: "Bah-bo–kee–vah–ree."

Although I've lived in southeastern Arizona for more than twenty years, I have yet to visit all her mountains. Even now, with leaving a real possibility, I'm not much inclined to make the effort. It would be the sort of artificial goal that has little appeal. I'm not setting records here, I'm living a life, and somehow its twists and turns have never taken me into the Santa Theresas, the Dos Cabezas, the Winchesters, or the Tortolitas. I know them only as blue lumps on the horizon or bits of type on a highway map. These ranges must have their aficionados, though: tireless hikers who have scrambled up every ridge and followed every creek bed; and even a few single–minded devotees who want to hear nothing of competing beauties across the state or across the valley. A bit of a chauvinist myself, I return again and again to a few well–loved places: the Santa Catalinas, the Pinaleños, the Huachucas, the Santa Ritas. What drives me is not curiosity to know what lies beyond that ridge or on top of the next peak. If it was, there would be no gaps on my list. Rather, what compels me is a yen for intimacy.

When I climb to the roof of my house, I am always startled at how quickly the horizon ends. Mountains surround the basin where I live, and even the lowest of them is tall enough to hide the valleys and mountains that lie beyond. In defining my space, mountains turn an infinite universe into a finite one. These are the boundaries in which you must live, they seem to say; this is the place you have made your own.

# 2

# the gate swings wide

How does it happen, making a place your own? This is the question running through my mind this Monday morning as I step out the door to go to work. The November day is gray and drizzly, and the thrum of traffic from Twenty–second Street is as insistent as a rock-'n'–roll backbeat. The streets are wet, puddled at the dips. Half the drivers have their windshield wipers on. The other half do not, perhaps as a matter of pride, or sheer denial. We live in a desert. It cannot be raining.

A three–light wait at Country Club and Broadway. Cars, like desert harvester ants, evidently mate and multiply in rainy weather. Today it will take me at least thirty minutes to get to work. My office is halfway up a rocky knoll on the far side of town. Tumamoc Hill, it is called, after the O'odham word for "horned lizard," although not many residents of Tucson know it by name or even realize it exists. The hill and its environs are a nature preserve and an outdoor laboratory, eight hundred acres of desert that have remained unspoiled for more than ninety years.

The first to arrive, I unlock the gate at the bottom of the hill and swing it open. The wet steel chills my hand. The hinges sing, and then there is silence.

I leave the gate open and head up the hill. My husband, who grew up on Puget Sound in western Washington, likes to say that he never needed to go to summer camp because, as he puts it, "I *lived* at summer camp." And he did, with access to a little creek for fishing, a vacant lot for ball games, the Sound itself for clamming and swimming, and woods for berry-picking. The same applies to me, more or less: I do not live at summer camp, but I am fortunate enough to work there. Betsy, the research ecologist with whom I share an office, says it like this: "It's Monday, and I *get* to come to work."

It is axiomatic that the first person to drive up the hill in the morning sees the best wildlife. In warmer weather a collared lizard sometimes basks at the edge of the roadway near the gate. These are gray-stippled lizards about a foot long when fully grown. Last summer, one ran into the road in front of my car and did several push-ups, asserting territorial dominance and a willingness to fight. Then, getting a better look at the sheer imposing mass of my car—I could almost see him blanch and gulp—he changed his mind and ran away.

Today, several coyotes file across the road about fifty feet ahead of me. They are golden brown animals with thin faces and bushy but lank tails. I catch up with them and stop, engine idling. One coyote stands closer to the road than the rest, a kind of guardian for the other four, which are playing in full view like puppies, rolling and nuzzling and pawing. The guardian and I stare at one another for a slow count of twenty, thirty, fifty seconds, as if mutually hypnotized. It is a common enough experience, but it gives me chills every time. Finally, the coyote, apparently satisfied, turns its head and trots off toward the others.

I drive halfway up the hill and park my car near one of the three stone buildings that belong to the Desert Laboratory. The lab was founded nearly a century ago to study desert plants and animals, especially their means of survival in an arid climate. We are still studying.

Before I forget, I enter my coyote sighting in the wildlife log, a spiral bound notebook in the main office. Most of the entries are brief—wildlife glimpsed on the run as we go about our daily business. In the log's pages, coyotes chew on mesquite leaves, a roadrunner kills and eats a small rattlesnake, two collared peccaries copulate, seven baby quail swim in the water hole, a Harris hawk attacks but misses an adult quail.

These unsystematic observations have little scientific value, yet if the log disappeared, I am certain that someone would start one again. And again, and again, as a necessary thing. Ecologist and entomologist Edward O. Wilson wrote a book called *Biophilia*. The title, derived from Greek roots meaning love of life, could mean almost anything: love of being alive, or love of one's own life, or love of the chemicals and processes that constitute life at the molecular level. The love of life that Wilson has in mind is love of animals other than ourselves. This is not the love we feel for a pet, which is more akin to our feelings for our children or our husbands and wives. Biophilia is a recognition of all we share with furred and winged and scaled creatures—beating hearts, mobile limbs, discriminating eyes and tongues, and familial responsibilities, to name a few. Biophilia is the instinctive understanding that I have more in common with a tail-flicking junco than either of us has with a chunk of granite. When we are out-of-doors, biophilia is what draws us to watch a mule deer watching us or to stare as a red-tailed hawk spirals upward in the sky. We are interested in these common animals because they are alive, and because we are alive, too.


The ground is soft from previous rains. My feet sink a full inch into the soil as I walk to the weather station. I dip the calibrated stick into the rain gauge, then pull it out. Nearly two-tenths of an inch of rain fell overnight and early this morning. Altogether, three inches have fallen since the middle of October, a bonanza after the unusually dry summer. Already people are talking about the possibility of a good spring, meaning a spring riotous with poppies and lupines and delphiniums. *A good spring*—that is the phrase we use. It sounds like a modest request—not a fabulous spring, please, nor a splendiferous one, merely a good spring will be fine—but, given the usual rainfall pattern of our winters, it is like asking for an early return of Halley's comet.

This autumn's rainfall has had more immediate consequences. A shadow of gray–green seedlings spreads under every brittlebush. A low shrub with felty white stems, brittlebush has cheerful yellow flowers the size of quarters. Last May the plants seeded abundantly, and despite the best efforts of house finches and harvester ants, much seed was left on the soil and in it. Now hundreds of thousands of brittlebush seedlings have emerged around the Desert Laboratory. This is a reasonably common event, much more common than the good spring for which all of us are hoping. In the last eight winters, brittlebush seedlings emerged in mass five times. All they need is seven–tenths of an inch of rain—a good, thorough soaking—to leach the germination inhibitors from the seed coats. Most desert annuals require twice that amount of water for germination.

Seeds of many woody plants around here germinate after summer rains—paloverde, mesquite, whitethorn acacia, ocotillo. I see paloverde seedlings almost every summer, mesquite and whitethorn seedlings less often, and ocotillo seedlings never. And yet, one summer ecologist Forrest Shreve saw countless numbers of ocotillo seedlings on these very slopes. Full–grown ocotillos have long, wand-like branches, sometimes a hundred or more in a single clump, and gaudy red flowers like torches. Forrest Shreve wrote, "The number of seedlings of this plant which appear during the few days of active germination is so great as to make it utterly impracticable to keep track of them."

What he did not realize, having lived in the desert only nine years at that point, was the rareness of this event. We now know that oco-tillo seeds need a heavy rain before they will germinate, at least an inch. Storms of this magnitude do not necessarily happen every summer. Also, birds and possibly other animals as well have vora-cious appetites for the seeds. In most years, the heaviest rains arrive after the seed crop has been consumed. Forrest Shreve witnessed a rare year in which heavy rains came early, allowing seedlings to emerge before animals ate the seeds.

I have not lived here all that long myself—only twenty-four years—and there is much I have not seen. I've seen enough, though, to know that the value of the Desert Laboratory increases with every decade because its records are a long memory that exceeds the span of most human lifetimes.

A photograph taken in 1906 of the original Desert Laboratory staff shows ten men in starched white shirts and ties, and two women in floor-length dresses, hair wrapped around their heads. They were lucky to be here, and they knew it. When a plant physiologist named Burton Livingston was offered laboratory space in 1907, he re-sponded, "This is the best thing that ever happened to yours truly." A co-worker, Francis Lloyd, was impressed by having "vegetation at the door, with all day and night one's own." William Cannon, the first ecologist on the premises, noted that laboratory researchers did not compete for projects; rather, the main problem was to choose among the abundance of possibilities.

Since Cannon's day, statistics and computers have revolutionized ecological research, but some things have not changed. I can still walk out the door of my office and be at one of my field sites in less than a minute. The abundance of problems to investigate is so great that ninety-odd years of research have not even come close to ex-hausting them. After ten years on Tumamoc Hill, I believe that com-ing here was among the best things that ever happened to me, too. It's hard to imagine that I might have to leave someday soon.

I remember my botanical forebears at odd moments—when I find a rusted forceps on a field plot, or when I handle their old and brittle vegetation maps. I know them well in some ways, not at all in others. Edith Shreve, Forrest Shreve's wife, was so devoted to her research that she worked without a salary or a budget of her own. Yet when her laboratory burned to the ground, destroying all her notes, she gave up her work—her life—without a backward glance. Jacob Blumer, who earned sixty dollars a year as the Desert Laboratory's research assistant in 1906, mapped every one of the ten thousand saguaros that grew on Tumamoc Hill. He had available to him only the rather primitive surveying equipment of the time, and it must have been an unendingly tedious and exacting task. Yet his colleague, Burton Livingston, mysteriously remarked that Blumer "made too hard work of things and failed to make much of his time, in my humble opinion." Their stories move me inexpressibly. Biophilia of another sort.

A transplant from Maryland, Forrest Shreve knew nothing about the desert on the day he arrived. He had kept himself in deliberate ignorance, and everything he saw was strange and unfamiliar, from the dust devils that swept across the plains to the prickly pears that seemed about to melt from midsummer's heat. Eventually, the desert took him in, or he took it in, with his research on desert plants. Hard to say which. You can recognize a landscape as home by making it into a place where you belong, or by making yourself into a person who belongs in that place.

I moved to Arizona with my first husband, Phil, when I was nineteen. I'd never lived anywhere but southern California, and I felt that I was going into exile. More than once I recalled a Bible story I had learned as a child in Sunday School, the story of Ruth and how, for the sake of her husband, she left her family and the only home she had ever known. My place is with my husband, she had said. I will go wherever he goes. I must have agreed, because that's exactly what I did; nevertheless, I felt exiled from all the familiar associations and sights that had attached me to the place I called home—vineyards, citrus groves, orange blossoms, blue-shouldered mountains.

What I missed most was the classic southern California landscape: rolling hills the color of a mountain lion's coat, ravines stuffed with dark green oaks, and skies as blue as lapis lazuli. It was a hypnotic landscape; I found it so as a child, anyway, and I wanted our long Sunday drives through the countryside never to end. To say that I missed this landscape after I moved to Arizona is to markedly understate the case. I ached for it, craved it, needed it as much as I needed sleep.

In medicine, when doctors cannot demonstrate that a certain type of infection is present yet strongly suspect that it is, they treat the patient with the appropriate medication, and if the infection disappears, the inference is that the patient did indeed have the disease in question. Phil and I moved to Arizona and I hated everything about it—the shabbiness, the aridity, the heat, the endless desert—until the day we drove south on the freeway, following the Santa Cruz River valley, and I saw for the first time the Santa Rita Mountains. I painted the scene in watercolors as soon as we got home, so I know quite well what I saw that day: distant blue peaks, green rolling foothills, and white clouds piled in a brilliant blue sky. Now that I know these mountains well, I see almost nothing in common between them and the grassy hills I knew as a child; but on that particular day, in that particular light, at that particular distance, the two landscapes converged in my mind. Suddenly I felt—not at home, that was to require more time—I felt not exiled at least, no longer Ruth among the alien corn. The cure proves the diagnosis; imprinted at a young age upon a particular landscape, I was a motherless child until I was returned to it again.

written on rock

One place that draws me back time after time is Signal Hill, a tilted wedge of solid granite that is, with infinite slowness, disintegrating in place. Although it is little more than a knoll, Signal Hill commands a sweeping view to the north, east and west, hundreds of miles of wide plains edged by dark blue mountains. What drew me here to-day, however, was not the view, fine though it is. I have come to see the designs pecked into the jumbled boulders on top of the hill. Al-most every smooth rock face has two or more designs—spirals, big-horn sheep, suns, stick men, ampersands, treble clefs, zigzags, criss-crossing lines—combined in no particular order that I can discern. Each drawing is a series of dots like a pointillist painting or a news-paper photograph, and each dot represents a strike or blow from a stone chisel. As always, I am struck by the fact that the farther away I stand, the clearer the designs. When I move too close, the patterns disappear into the roughness of the rock.

Made by the Hohokam Indians who once inhabited the area, these petroglyphs are about a thousand years old. The Hohokam were farmers and potters: their irrigation canals still crisscross the desert in places, and any excavation around town, even for a vegetable bed, is apt to turn up shards of earthen-colored pottery.

Where freshly exposed, Signal Hill granite is pale gray or tan. Otherwise it is darkly varnished with magnesium and other chemicals precipitated from the rock. The drawings are recent enough to contrast vividly with the varnish. How satisfying this must have been to the ancient artist, the pale figures emerging from a black surface. I find it satisfying, anyway, and unexpectedly I remember being a child just learning to print with a soft-leaded pencil between wide-spaced blue lines. For the briefest of moments I feel the satisfaction of watching the black letters form on thin sheets of newsprint and of being the one who put them there.

It is a brilliant winter day—blue skies, landscape awash with warmth and light—the kind of day that almost makes up for the intolerable desert summers. There was frost on the grass when I left home this morning, but desert days warm up quickly in December, and it is cozy here among the sun-warmed boulders.

In midsummer, with bright sun washing out every nuance and shadow, the Tucson Mountains seem perfectly flat and smooth. Now winter's slanting light reveals their curves and hollows, somehow shaping sculpture out of two dimensions, as if you were to create a globe by wrapping a map of the world around a beach ball. A gently sloping plain rises from the valley floor to the base of the Tucson Mountains; it is called a *bajada,* from the Spanish word for descent or slope. Stretched across the bajada is the lightest, thinnest veil of green possible to imagine, a fine, green gauze woven from saguaros and paloverdes and other desert plants. The view is green because of bark, not leaf—the yellow-green bark of paloverde, the blue-green skin of saguaro and prickly pear.

The steep south side of Signal Hill is where the smoothest rock faces are as well as most of the drawings. I wander among them like a patron in a museum, sketchbook in hand. Two spirals are placed side by side, one about the size of a dinner plate, the other no wider than the palm of my hand: around and around they go, diving into their own centers. On a flat surface nearby, a sun drawing faces the sky, one sun staring at another. My favorite is a human figure, obviously male. His curved arms are raised up, like a saguaro; his curved legs are their mirror image. A head pokes up between the arms, and a penis dangles between the legs. If you turned him on end, he would look no different, which is why he amuses me.

In Canyon de Chelly in northeastern Arizona, there's a petroglyph panel called Newspaper Rock. Placed high on a smooth sandstone wall, the drawings are accessible by tumbled rocks and a narrow ledge. Many years ago, I stood on that ledge and made rubbings with rice paper and charcoal pencils. I have them still: bighorn sheep with legs splayed like rocking horses, and flute players as wistful and haunting as a whippoorwill's call. In those days, I fantasized living a life such as I imagined the Anasazi had led: free and natural and easy, bedding down like bears in caves and shelters, climbing hand over hand up rock walls as slick as glass, running down deer and rabbit, savoring the wild fruits of the earth. My fantasy, like many such, romanticized their life past all recognition, an expression of my needs, not theirs.

There are many Newspaper Rocks in the Southwest. They have in common a jumble and profusion of art, less like a newspaper, really, than a ransom note assembled from letters cut out of magazines—a wild and unpredictable assortment of typefaces and fonts. Here on Signal Hill, zigzags, spoked wheels, and six–legged creatures crowd together, even overlap. Bighorn sheep leap toward complicated geometric designs. Wavy lines underscore blazing suns. We call them "newspapers" because that is the handiest analogy, but actually no one knows their purpose.

Perhaps the oddest thing about ancient rock art is the way a few signs crop up again and again in widely separated localities. Almost simultaneously, it seems, many different pairs of hands in many different places were chiseling identical deer as methodically as a car–

toonist recreates his characters every day. This curious uniformity suggests that rock art was not—or not only—self-expression; surely some more standard mode of communication was involved.

Many Hohokam petroglyphs are abstract designs of spirals and circles found on crests of hills or rock outcroppings. According to a Park Service plaque at the base of Signal Hill, "the meaning and placement of these artworks remain a mystery. Were they signs of celebration, part of the planting rituals, a calendar, or markers for hunting routes?" Good question. What I want to know, though, is whether they are text or art. If art, they are not complex enough to hold my interest; if text, I could happily spend days or years decoding them. That's my bias—an automatic fealty to written words rather than visual images. Maybe they are both. I try to imagine living in a culture that makes no distinction between the two, but find it as inconceivable as tasting with my hands or smelling with my ears.

Strolling among the boulders, I think the usual thoughts about what it means to write on rock and then to be read nine hundred years later. The last of these Hohokam artist-farmers were contemporaneous with Chaucer. That their drawings conveyed meaning at one time we can scarcely doubt. To incise a single spiral required a thousand blows—hardly the work of a moment or a whim. No matter, their messages are silent, now. Our writings could prove equally ephemeral. If not for a sturdy tradition of Middle English scholarship, we might have lost Chaucer already. In another nine hundred years, the length of time since the Hohokam incised these patterns, perhaps no one will be able to decipher our signs, either.


The Hohokam required nothing more than what the desert itself provided in order to survive. To construct a new house, they scooped out a good-sized room in alluvial silt, gave it sturdy corner posts, then thatched it with brush and plastered it with mud. In some places, they farmed by irrigation; the Santa Cruz and Rillito Rivers flowed year-round then, and the Hohokam dug short canals from the rivers to their fields. Their crops were corn, beans, cotton, and squash. At other places, the Hohokam farmed by harvesting floodwater. They plugged up small arroyos with brush and stones, then waited for the summer rains. The first flash flood of the season washed down a rich organic mulch of decayed leaves and rotted twigs, all of which was trapped behind the weir of brush and rock. There, in the recently enriched and newly moistened soil, they planted their crops. Successive floods and rains provided the rest of the required moisture.

Even in good years, the Hohokam needed wild plants as well as crops. Mesquite pods, ground into flour and baked, or eaten green and sweet, were a staple. Succulent saguaro fruits were boiled down into a thick, sweet syrup used in making wine. Wolfberry, prickly pear, hackberry, manzanita, oak—all had fruits that the Hohokam harvested and relished. In drought years, wild plants might be their only source of sustenance. In any year, good or bad, they looked to the desert for fibers for weaving sandals and baskets, needles for sewing rabbit skins into blankets, gum for mending broken pots, soap for washing hair and skin.

You might think, on the face of it, that they were like the perennials that endure the desert all year, while we are like the drought-escaping ephemerals that appear only in the coolest, wettest months. Charles Bowden, thinking of how we demand much—cars, gasoline, air conditioners, refrigerators, electricity—where the aboriginal peoples needed little, wrote, "Suddenly I know I am not of this place and do not belong here and that there is no study of ecology or botany, no bath in some thing called nature that will alter this fact. There is no process of modifying my behavior, no simple environmental checklist that will render me into something that fits into this baked ground." There is some truth to this. But we are here, no? and the Hohokam are not. The triumph of the last, or at least the latest—we may comment on them rather than they on us, a kind of chronological imperialism.

The Anasazi eventually abandoned their beautiful cliff dwellings for reasons that remain essentially a mystery. We can make educated guesses based on inference—that there was a regional drought is certain, and that it was worse than any drought the Anasazi had experienced within living memory seems likely—but exactly how they expressed these facts to themselves we will never know. Perhaps they felt that their gods had abandoned them. The decision to pack up and move could have been the decision to find the new dwelling place of the gods. Or perhaps, more disgusted than frightened, the Anasazi decided to consign the old gods to the dry and dusty fields and to seek out new gods in moister, more fertile ground. Either way, the emotional cost of leaving the only homeland they had ever known must have been great, requiring, I would guess, an extremely powerful rationalization.

The same regional drought would have affected the Hohokam, too. Because they were already adapted to life in the desert, they might have been better prepared to handle drought than the Anasazi; on the other hand, their technology was more oriented toward evading and accommodating aridity than conquering it. In any case, during the eleventh and twelfth centuries the Hohokam too began to leave villages that had been continuously occupied for hundreds of years.

To my mind, this must have been a shattering experience. I have left places before, and it has never been easy. My attachments to places, in fact, have long been stronger than most of my attachments to people. I imagine that the attachment of the Anasazi and Hohokam to their ancestral lands must have been equally intense. How could it be otherwise? Where to find medicinal plants and basketry materials, where to dig for clay, where to find fresh drinking water during the driest part of the year, the kind of practical information that had been gathered through many generations—almost everything they knew had its basis in where they lived. Geographic facts that they had always taken for granted—the direction of the prevailing winds, the amount of rain and its seasonality, the length of the growing season, the sharpness of winter frosts—would be of little use in a foreign place. Even the conformation of the stars they saw at night depended upon being in one place rather than another.

The desert has claimed much of what the Hohokam left behind. Their brush houses and ramadas have collapsed, a bonanza for desert termites. Their ball courts have been sifted over with dirt, their floodwater fields with rocks and sticks and other debris. The romantic in me wants to praise their gentle sojourn in this place, a tenure not harmful to the earth.

They could hardly live out of balance: the desert is not an environment that encourages profligacy. Just as the wolfberry wears its tiny leaves only when the soil is wet, otherwise conserving its precious resources, so the desert peoples led lives of careful calculation. They knew it would be a long time between the life–giving rains of one summer and the next. They had learned through painful centuries how to outlast the rainless days of late spring by accumulating stores of wild and cultivated foods; but the desert always circumscribed their efforts and their lives.

Today, we admit no circumscriptions at all, and when we are gone, our passage will prove to have been harsh. Steel, asphalt, glass, and plastic will not dissolve in a termite's gut. If you examine our way of life from an ecological perspective, it is almost impossible to avoid the conclusion that, as Bowden said, we are not of this place.

But we must occupy some spot of ground. If not here, then where? And, from an evolutionary perspective, it makes little sense to exalt the Hohokam at our expense. As Edward O. Wilson noted, "Genetic advantage accrued from planned modifications of the environment." Our ancestors, in other words, fiddling around with rocks, branches, dirt, and twigs, figured out how to erect shelters, harness fire, and make tools. In doing so, they improved their quality of life and increased their chances of surviving to the age of sexual maturity. Their offspring inherited not the knowledge of how to make a stone axe or a brush shelter but the intelligence and dexterity to do so.

All human culture involves technology of some sort, whether basketry or plastic–injected molding. The Hohokam and ourselves are not opposites but points on a continuum. If this desert has too little water to sustain five hundred thousand human lives, we will siphon distant rivers. The Hohokam did much the same, only on a smaller scale. If the frugal soil cannot produce enough food, we will import it by truck and train. What are our grocery stores but a modern version of a storage jar filled with grain? The problem is that technology is adaptive until it becomes maladaptive. At Chaco Canyon in northeastern New Mexico, Anasazi Pueblos of the eighth century grew so large and demanded so much timber that they eventually extirpated ponderosa pine from the nearby mesa tops. We are genetically programmed to modify our environment but not, it seems, to call a halt when we have gone too far.

The question is not whether we will consume resources and blot the landscape. Being human, we assuredly will. The question is how much do we need to consume, how big a blot must we make? If we have more technology than we need, the Hohokam perhaps had too little. For them, as for us, technology is a kind of carapace, as much a part of who we are and how we live as the turtle's shell or the packrat's den.

My sketchbook is overflowing: wavy lines, triple arches, cogwheels, curious Celtic knots, irresistible bighorn sheep. Art or text? I will never know. All I know is that Homo sapiens is the recording animal, and either way, these symbols are a kind of technology, as much so as clay pots, irrigation canals, and grocery stores.

Here and there the granite is spalling away where rainwater has seeped into hairline cracks, then frozen. Thin layers of ice expand, acting as wedges, pushing the outer shell of rock until it breaks off. These drawings have withstood a thousand years of rain and frost, but they will not last forever. That I scribble sketches of them and assemble words about them proves what we already knew: our need-to-make outlasts the things made.

# a tango with bears

4

Near the Ramsey Canyon trail head, a bucket of water hangs from a post. The lower reaches of the canyon belong to The Nature Conservancy, and you're supposed to snuff out your cigarettes before you start up the trail. Fine, except that on this chilly January day you'd have to drill a hole first, because the water in the bucket is frozen solid. Hard to believe Steve and I are only seventy miles and one month from the sun-washed petroglyphs on Signal Hill.

Ramsey Canyon heads high in the Huachuca Mountains. On a map, its steep upper reaches resemble the splayed-out fingers of a hand. In summer, the canyon bottom is a cool and shaded place: sycamores and maples along the stream, several kinds of oak and pine on the slopes. When the trees are fully leaved, their canopy is so dense that you cannot see the mountain crest upstream. Ramsey Canyon, then, seems to exist in isolation, a green declivity with no beginning and no end. But in winter, when brown cliffs are visible between the bare, white branches, you cannot help seeing how, as Mary Austin put it, canyons are the streets of the mountains.

Puddles on the trail, like the cigarette bucket, are iced over. When I step on one, it shatters into large, jagged pieces. Beside the trail, the stream runs freely. I try to imagine it as solid ice but fail. My experience with real winters is so limited that I have never seen a frozen river, never seen trees sparkle after an ice storm, never sledded down a hill or even a steep driveway. I remember a family trip to the mountains long ago when my sister and I made snow angels. I doubt that we owned mittens or rubber boots, for I recall being surprised at the icy wetness of snow on my hands and feet.

The Ramsey Canyon trail begins as an old road now closed to vehicles. Today it is thickly plastered with snow that has been beaten down by hikers. Every footprint has a polished, icy surface, so Steve and I stay close to the edge of the road where we can walk on untrodden snow. It crunches underfoot in a satisfying fashion. "The sound of compaction," Steve observes. The crunch feels as good under my boot as it does in my ear.

Back in the woods, the snow is splotched with holes like a ragged T-shirt, showing leaves as brown as skin. The entire landscape is splotchy, in fact: the trunks of sycamores are blotched in shades of gray and cream and white like monochrome giraffes; the sky is mottled in other, darker, grays; and the cliffs are variegated with chartreuse and yellow lichens.

We haven't gone twenty feet before I find a little bird, dead, at the roadside. Its downy plumage is olive green and gray, its bill a short, black spike. An immature warbler of some sort. Steve guesses that it died from cold and lack of food. "Should have migrated months ago," he says. Will the trail be littered from this point onward with the bodies of small, frozen birds? I remember what I learned as a child in Sunday school, that not a sparrow falls but God notices it. I wanted to believe that this meant God would prevent all harm from coming to sparrows and small girls, but even then I knew better. Now, winter seems inimical to life, a kind of silent, white predator.

Heart-shaped tracks of deer crisscross the snowy flats. A caretaker at the visitor center told us that deer are numerous and obvious in Ramsey Canyon this winter. "The males have been showing off for the females," she said. Deer move down mountains in the wintertime in search of food. They are browsing animals, especially in winter when there is no fresh, green herbage. We sometimes see them nibbling on low branches of oak or mountain mahogany, thoughtfully tugging off a few leaves at a time, chewing them well, then tugging off a few more. Winter is the lean time for deer, and many more starve than succumb to mountain lions and other predators. The problem is not lack of food as such, but lack of nutritious food. Browse plants tends to be lowest in protein and minerals during the winter. Not uncommonly, deer die of malnourishment with their stomachs full of food.

Mountain lions, which feed mainly on deer, follow their prey down mountains in winter, so it is exciting but not surprising when Steve finds among the deer tracks a different kind of imprint in the snow. Each print is as wide as the palm of my hand and consists of a foot pad and four toes. Their huge size, combined with the lack of claw marks, suggests mountain lion to both of us. I automatically look up, hoping to see a lion crouched on a branch overhead, but no luck. "Never any top carnivores around when you want them," Steve says philosophically.

Exceptions to this rule tend to provide as much adrenaline as satisfaction. Last summer, Steve and I encountered a bear, a shaggy, cinnamon-colored adult, not too far from here. On the rare occasions when we see bears, they are usually departing the scene, a good thing for all concerned. This time, however, the bear was unwilling to budge. Our presence seemed to make it restless and uneasy. The bear turned in small circles like a dog preparing to nap, then hunkered down beside the trail. As we watched it, an odd noise, rather like a bellows expelling air, attracted my attention. I looked in the direction of the sound and saw another bear, larger than the first and black instead of brown, on a slope to our left. My amazement at seeing two adult bears together was somewhat tempered by the demeanor of the second bear: planted on all four feet, head down, shoulders hunched, it was huffing and puffing like the wolf in *The Three Little Pigs*. Having read that bears often try to bluster their way out of a fight, I was only mildly alarmed; at the same time, I was not inclined to call its bluff. In any case, the first bear was plainly determined to stand its ground, which meant that our hike had reached an end, if not *the* end.

As we headed back the way we came, Steve stopped abruptly. "I want to photograph it, if I can," he said. We reversed direction and shuffled up the trail until we saw the first bear, which was right where we had left it, directly ahead at a distance of about forty yards. It decided to retreat and lumbered up the trail, pausing frequently to turn and look at us. Emboldened by the bear's apparent timidity, Steve shuffled after it, a few steps at a time. I shuffled after Steve. Soon we were directly downslope of the second bear, which was a very large bear indeed. We inched a little closer, then a little more. Steve held his camera to his eye and turned the focusing ring. The second bear growled.

"But Steve," I said, "what about the other bear?"

"The *other* bear?"

I pointed at it, whereupon we beat a hasty but dignified retreat.

Many months later, Steve asked me, "What in the world was going through your mind?" It's hard to say. In all likelihood, I thought Steve knew about both animals as we crept back up the trail. Only when death and destruction loomed perilously close did I understand that he had not seen the second bear. Even then, reluctant to second-guess him, I phrased my doubts as tactfully as possible. I have many flaws, but at least no one can impugn my loyalty.

Later I learned that we had probably interrupted the bears' courtship. This explained much that had been mysterious: it takes two to tango, after all, and most of us would be uneasy and tentative with a partner capable of ripping out our guts. Finding a compatible mate is doubtless no easier for bears than humans; having gone to a world of trouble to pair off, our ursine couple was forced to set romance aside as they watched two foolhardy human beings, one apparently blind and deaf, the other clearly mute, execute an impromptu two-way shuffle in the middle of the dance floor. No wonder they seemed irritated and confused.

As we gain altitude, the patches of snow coalesce into a continuous fabric. The ground is humpbacked with snowy logs, and every stump wears a beefeater's cap of snow. Until an acorn woodpecker appears on a tall snag, the only touches of brightness in the landscape are green patches of moss. Through binoculars I can see the woodpecker's clown face, painted in black and white, and its bright bellboy's cap, a perfect circle of red. It drums vigorously against the wood.

Even from this distance, I can tell that the snag is perforated like a Chinese checkers board and that almost every hole contains an acorn. The tree seems to have a hundred brown eyeballs. This is the woodpecker's kitchen cupboard. Acorn woodpeckers are cooperative breeders and live in family groups of a dozen or so birds. All members of the group construct nest holes, care and feed for nestlings, defend a five-acre territory, gather food. Their acorn storage trees—granaries, they are called—are handed down from generation to generation and eventually accumulate enormous numbers of storage holes, more than thirty thousand in some trees. Woodpeckers probably started filling the holes of this granary in August and September, when the acorns of netleaf and silverleaf oak began to ripen, and continued through October and November, when Arizona oak acorns become plentiful. Now that winter has cut off other food sources such as sap and flying insects, their efforts pay off.

Curiously, the number of holes in a good-sized granary—about thirty thousand—is close to the number of acorns a mature Arizona oak produces each year. This is *not* what is meant by the balance of nature, however. A jay might bury five thousand acorns in a season but is likely to recover and eat only one third of them. The other two thirds may well germinate and grow into fine new oaks. Unlike jays, acorn woodpeckers remove acorns from the reproductive cycle entirely. Like bankers who assume that a certain proportion of loans will be uncollectable, oaks must figure irrecoverable losses into their total seed production.

Innumerable small objects litter the snow: lobed leaves of Gambel oak, both green and brown; needles of white fir, also green and brown; acorns, some single, some joined nape to nape like Siamese twins. The acorns are the last of this year's crop. Bad timing on their part, to fall onto fresh snow where birds and squirrels are bound to see them. Acorns are nutritious food, with a high proportion of carbohydrate and fat and more protein than most cereals. They make up fifteen percent of the diet of the Arizona gray squirrel, second only to walnuts, and half or more of the diets of the acorn woodpecker, the gray-breasted jay, the Steller's jay and the band-tailed pigeon. In some years, these and other birds and mammals consume as much as sixty-five percent of the acorn crop. In other years, grubs of various sorts might ruin fifty percent. Sometimes the crop is virtually a total loss, with eight of ten acorns being destroyed in one way or another.

Not to worry, however; the oak has a master plan, which involves producing bounteous acorn crops in some years, niggardly crops in others, a kind of feast-and-famine routine. If every year were a bountiful year, acorn eaters—especially grubs—would multiply without restraint. The solution? Mix good years with bad. In the bad years, acorn eaters cannot breed with abandon, and their populations remain low. They may, however, consume most of the niggardly crop. In the good years, their populations—suppressed by the series of bad years—are still small, but the crop is so bountiful that they cannot possibly consume it all. These are the years when, if rains are adequate, acorns are most likely to become seedlings.

The farther we hike, the less trodden the path. Now only two pairs of footprints precede ours. Snow leaks into the tops of our hiking boots with every step. The heavy clouds, which have been threatening rain all morning, finally let loose a flurry of frozen raindrops. They sizzle like high-tension wires in fog.

We soon enter a zone where the skin of snow has pulled back to reveal the richly colored forest floor—the cinnamony red of pine needles, the rich browns of oak leaves, the umbers and blacks of rotted bark. How brilliant all these so-called earth tones are when displayed on a white backdrop.

Brown and brittle wildflowers, mementos of summer, poke above the snow. I recognize *Helianthella* by its spherical heads, now empty of seed, and *Scrophularia* from its big panicles and tiny capsules. They remind me of how these slopes looked five months ago. Then yellow wildflowers bloomed under the pines, grasses and sedges grew thick at streamside, and branches of bigtooth maple spread above them in layer upon layer of greenery. Oddly, I feel that I cannot really *see* the landscape now because of the snow. It is like reading a poem in which all the allusions are to myths and stories I have not read. Nor do I have any idea how to see the snow itself, no idea at all. I have no words for it, for one thing, and seeing snow—or any natural feature—is partly a matter of vocabulary. Knowing the words for a phenomenon helps you see it better, or at least differently. The best I can do now is peruse the poem again and again, hoping some of its meaning sinks in.

Snow falls so silently, I expect these woods to be silent too, but they are not. There's the constant static of our boots crunching the snow, the drumming of another acorn woodpecker, the self-absorbed chatter of a canyon wren as it searches for insects in bedrock crevices. The wren jabs its bill into a slender horizontal crack, runs along the rock, jabs again. In winter, insect life is at its lowest ebb, forcing most songbirds to migrate south. The dead warbler we saw earlier did not, and winter harvested its life. The few birds that stay behind must rely heavily on stored food, like the acorn woodpecker, or, like the canyon wren, on whatever grubs they can scavenge from soil and bark. A snow cover lasting more than a few days could mean starvation for canyon wrens and other insect eaters.

The trail swings close to a wall of gray rock. Clear ice ripples down it in frozen flow. Pendant icicles make a thick and spiky fringe along the ledges. Some are blunt cylinders up to a foot long, others tenuous threads like blown glass. Along the stream, dangling roots are encased in ice wherever water splashes them. A few water striders skate on the shivering pools. Their front legs are clawed, for grasping prey, their mouthparts are beaked, for piercing and sucking. Like every other predator, they are precisely equipped to capture and kill. Ordinarily they eat aquatic insects that stray to the surface and terrestrial insects that fall into the water, but I cannot imagine what food they are finding on this frigid day.

An acorn woodpecker flies down the trail ahead of us, a swooping black bird in a snowy landscape. Disappearing into the trees it yells, "Jacob, Jacob, Jacob." Or so my field guide describes its call. To me it sounds more like bedsprings protesting as a child jumps up and down on a mattress. The acorn woodpecker, with its hoard of acorns, has a better chance of surviving the winter than the canyon wren, but it pays a price. Hoards of any sort require defense, and acorn woodpeckers spend a substantial proportion of their time in chasing thieves away from the granary. An aerial pass or two drives away almost any bird, but squirrels are more persistent. One observer saw five acorn woodpeckers make seventy-three passes at a squirrel which, undeterred, finally extracted an acorn and ran away.

Hoards require maintenance, too. Because the number of acorns that can be stored each autumn depends on the number of holes available, the birds that guard the granary must spend their free time drilling new holes. And, because the acorns shrink as they dry, the woodpeckers must reinsert them in tighter holes. Not my idea of a good job, a winter spent in moving innumerable acorns from one hole to another. Thus the circle completes itself: a seasonally abundant source of food encourages hoarding, then the hoarders become slaves to their hoard.

Thinking about woodpecker granaries, which tie generations of woodpeckers to five particular acres of ground, I wonder if there is an invisible biological underpinning to our human love of place. Although we tend to forget the fact, we are mammals after all, and almost every mammal has a home range, an area where it searches for food, and within its home range, a territory, a smaller area that it occupies and defends. Its place. Territories make powerful biological sense. By confining most of its activities to a circumscribed area, an animal learns where the safest hiding places are and where food is most likely to be found. It thereby conserves energy and prolongs its life. There is a powerful psychological benefit, too. An animal is strongest on its own territory—more able to repel enemies and assert its needs. Thus, the biological reasons for getting to know one place well are strong. The wonder is that any of us ever it leave for someplace else.

My territory, to be absolutely literal about it, consists of a small city lot, a tiny piece of ground compared to the five acres an acorn woodpecker shares with its kin. In the twelve years I have lived on it, I've come to know it reasonably well, although there are some spots I've never been, such as the narrow strip of ground between the tool shed and the fence, a weedy, stickery place from which my cat extracts an endless succession of lizards. My home range is much more extensive. It includes all the routes I drive on a regular basis, and it includes my car, too. It encompasses Tumamoc Hill, where I work, and the grocery stores and cafes where I forage for food. In the broadest possible sense, my home range runs several hundred miles to the east and west of my house, another hundred to the north and south. Wherever saguaros mingle with paloverdes, wherever gray–breasted jays bounce from oak to oak, wherever I can name at least 80 percent of the plants around me, that's where I'm at home.

Unlike the gray–breasted jay and the acorn woodpecker, who are perfectly suited to this woodland and would perish if forced to live in a drastically different habitat, I could theoretically survive any-where—Anchorage or Austin, Sacramento or Seattle. That, in part, is what it means to be human. Homo sapiens is the species that, by vir-tue of technology it has created, can make a home for itself in almost any environment. But making a home and being at home in it are two different things. If I moved to another part of the country, I could establish a new legal territory as easily as I could buy or rent a house, but to feel at home there would require some time, maybe several years, and there is no guarantee that I would not in some ways al-ways feel like an exile.

Our feet and legs sink shin-deep in the snowy trail. We have climbed high enough to see the ridgeline of the Huachuca Moun-tains. The forest burned some years ago, and now the colors are white and black and gray: the snowy slopes, the matchstick trees, the leaden sky. By now, our boots and socks are soaking wet, and our feet are cold. Thinking about dry socks and hot coffee, we head back toward the car. On the way, I notice the dead warbler again. It should have left but for some reason it stayed behind and in doing so for-feited altogether the opportunity to go.

"Sure, I'd miss living here," Steve says when I ask him, "but . . ." He leaves the sentence unfinished. But that's not the only consideration, he means. He means that we can be happy living almost anyplace, whereas the number of cities where we can both find satisfying work in our fields is limited. Like migratory birds that must depart every autumn in search of warmth and plentiful food, we cannot neces-sarily stay put, not if we want to earn a living. This is a hard truth, which I resist. Surely he will get tenure. The alternative, like this wintry landscape, is so densely veiled that I cannot see it at all.

# 5

# too cold for comfort but not for joy

Several hundred feet above the bottom of Sabino Canyon, the Phone Line Trail follows the same contour for almost its entire length, tracking in and out of every side gully and ravine like a conscientious snail. This was one of my favorite trails until several years ago, when, like a much-loved book read once too often, it went dead on me. Nothing about it excited or moved me any longer. I had the good sense to let it alone for a while, and being here now is like a surprise meeting with someone I love unreservedly—my husband or my daughter—when my heart leaps like a happy dog from the jolt of recognition and joy.

Sometimes I wish I could start over at that point when each trail in these mountains was as mysterious as the next and the Catalina Highway was only a rumor. I would like to see it all again with fresh vision and that initial astonishment that such wildness could exist in my own backyard.

At the beginning, uncertain how to penetrate the high blue wall of the Santa Catalina Mountains, I besieged them in my own timid way. On weekends, my first husband and I would drive up Campbell Avenue or Swan Road, major boulevards that ended abruptly at the base of the mountains. Exploration, I called it, remembering Girl Scout outings where I had ambled up and down wooded slopes and splashed across shallow, rocky creeks. Once there, though, surrounded by private property, Phil was reluctant to trespass, and there was nothing for us to do but stand and look. Eventually, someone at a party mentioned that there were hiking trails up there. Hiking trails and a road. The siege was over.

Thinking of those epic, day-long hikes when, footsore and exhausted, we staggered down from the mountains at last, I inevitably recall the same three lines of a poem by Edna St. Vincent Millay: "we were very tired/ we were very merry/ we had gone back and forth all night on the ferry." Except that *we* had stridden up and down the mountain in seven-league boots, turned routes into trails and trails into super-highways, encompassed peaks, streams, cliffs, and ravines. We were the mountain, and she was us.

That's how I remember it, anyway. But knowing that Phil and I eventually parted with pain and distrust on his side, guilt and defiance on mine, I wonder if the memory is true. I wonder too about the bond that permits love for a place to outlast love for a person. How can one be so strong, the other so weak?

A late winter storm has lodged itself securely in this corner of the state, reminding me that ours is a climate of variable abundance. Plenty of heat, at times; plenty of cold, at times; plenty of rain, at times, and plenty of drought, also at times. And no predicting, except in the most general terms, when any of it will happen. Today, gray clouds clog the sky. The canyon itself is wildly, almost tastelessly, romantic, as full of clouds as a teakettle with steam. Along the ridges, streamers of mist wrap every knob and spire. For years, having read of English painters longing for the clarity of Mediterranean air, I wanted to see this marvelous light for myself, not realizing that I lived in it every day. Or almost every day, since this is definitely English air today, moist and soft and muffling.

But not an English landscape. This prospect is too assertively spiny for the British Isles. The saguaros, tall cacti with arms reaching skyward, are vertically striped with stiff, gray spines. The paloverdes, small trees shrink-wrapped in green bark, look innocuous enough, but every twig ends in a sharp thorn. The catclaw acacias, sturdy shrubs with spreading branches, are named for curved thorns that snag in skin or clothing. They dig deep, draw blood.

Spines are modified leaves, and thorns are modified stems; most desert plants are equipped with one or the other, and some are armed with both. *Armed:* that is the actual word that botanists use, as if an encounter with the desert is necessarily an adversarial experience. I try to picture a desert where thorns, like leaves, are deciduous. A kinder, gentler desert, except that you wouldn't dare go barefoot, that's for certain.

Spiny plants are plentiful along the Phone Line Trail; even so, it is rock that dominates the scene. Above and below me are wobbly cliffs like haphazardly stacked encyclopedias. Across the canyon, massive slabs of rock and isolated boulders are inserted more or less at random into the slopes. From an airplane you would not be aware of the vegetation, due to the paucity of leaves. Right now, some plants have no leaves at all: the paloverdes discarded their leaflets in the autumn, and the catclaws dropped theirs after the first hard frost. Their leaves are small, like those of most desert trees and shrubs, and many times dissected into minuscule leaflets, ideal for deserts. Tiny leaves can be produced rapidly and cheaply when the soil is wet, then discarded with few regrets once the soil dries out. At any season, they need less water than big leaves, and on the hottest days, they are less apt to scorch and die. The result, as now, is a plant community that seems to be defined by a great abundance of negative space.

Snowflakes, driven in bursts, swirl out of the sky and sting my face and hands. Some lines from an A. E. Housman poem pop into my head: "about the woodlands I will go to see the cherry hung with snow." That's why I'm here today, as a matter of fact: as inevitably as poets flock to cherry trees, I am drawn to see the snow. And anything else that catches my attention. Even in this familiar landscape, I could, if I am lucky, wander down new paths of thought.

Ordinarily, snow is as rare in the desert as cacti in Vermont. If I put my mind to it, I could probably recall every snowstorm in the twenty years since I moved here. When it snows in Tucson, we all pile into our cars and drive around to look at it. Objects so familiar that they had become invisible—railroad tracks, brick walls, tile roofs—leap to notice when transformed by snow. Oh, we say, this is what a rail fence looks like in the snow, a stack of flower pots, a coil of garden hose, a cement bird bath. John Jerome says, "What one wants is not the new but the re-newed, to find a way of renewing. You want to find a way to see freshly what has become unbearably old." That's what snow does for desert dwellers.

Today the saguaros, arms upraised, seem to be warding off the snow. Like most desert plants, they can take some cold but not a lot. In 1971, the coldest winter in twenty-two years, many full-grown saguaros on these slopes died of frost. To someone from Minnesota or Maine, the killing temperatures might sound laughably mild: the coldest night that winter was seventeen degrees Fahrenheit. But for saguaros, which evolved millions of years ago in the subtropics, it was a disastrous frost. Its effects were especially pronounced for two reasons: there were four unusually cold nights in a row, and on several of those nights, freezing temperatures lasted for twelve hours or longer.

Forrest Shreve was the first person to demonstrate the sensitivity of saguaros to cold. In 1910, he potted up small saguaros not much bigger than spaghetti squash, poked thermometers in them, and stuck them in a freezer for different lengths of time. This was well before the days of electric freezers; he used a contraption that cooled via ice and salt, like an old-fashioned ice cream freezer. (His was by and large a homely sort of science, the kind I like best, requiring little more than tape measure, clipboard, and occasionally some flower pots.) What he learned from this experiment, he reported, confirmed what he had observed in nature: the saguaro cannot withstand twenty-four consecutive hours of freezing temperatures. In the years since, no one has changed or even substantially improved upon this finding.


For a mile or more, a jutting promontory has blocked my view up the canyon. Walking past it now, I see more cliffs, rough towers sculpted in misty gray rock, and snow flying in front of them this way and that, the drifting flakes at the mercy of the wind. My fingers ache with cold inside thick Ragg gloves. I must keep moving to stay warm. While snow is not yet sticking to the ground, I suspect it will before long. The soil—what there is of it—is damp, and the rocks are wet and slick. Already, clumps of moss are turning from black to green as they soak up this chilly moisture.

The coldest temperature ever reported in Tucson was six degrees Fahrenheit during a January storm in 1913. Thousands of small saguaros were killed outright. Many large plants, some of them still around today, were damaged at the apex, where new tissue forms. Growth stopped or slowed for a couple of years, leaving a prominent and permanent constriction in the stem.

Saguaro populations eventually recover from catastrophic freezes. The process is slow and lengthy, though. Mature plants produce seeds in abundance, but most are devoured by ants, rodents, and birds before they can germinate with the first heavy summer rains. Seedling saguaros become established only with great reluctance: rabbits, ground squirrels, and packrats eat the newly germinated seedlings; cows trample them flat; hot days in summer fry them; cold nights in winter shrivel them. You could spend every summer for five years on your hands and knees looking for newly germinated saguaros and not find a single one.

To lose an entire generation of small plants to a single frost is a catastrophe indeed. With reasonable accuracy you can determine the age of a saguaro from its height, and a biologist measuring saguaro populations around Tucson would be struck by the absence of fifty-five- to sixty-year-old plants. This cohort was wiped out by the frost of 1937. It's reminiscent of the devastation brought by World War I, when an entire generation of young men was lost. Fortunately, populations rebound, and in the Santa Catalina Mountains and elsewhere, small saguaros are once again common. Given the right conditions, even great devastation can be undone or, if not quite that, at least reversed.

The snow thickens. Flakes clump together as they fall. It's like being pelted with shredded quilt batting. When I stop moving, I can hear it splat on my jacket and on the ground. Because the trail weaves in and out as it crosses one side canyon after another, I walk two miles to travel one. I would be glad to stop and rest but am too cold. Inside my wet gloves, my hands feel as if they will shatter. I'm no better adapted to cold weather than the saguaro. How would I fare if we moved to Maine or Minnesota?

Steve and I did consider moving to Montana once. We were crossing the Beartooth Range on the Montana–Wyoming border at the time. It was autumn, and the fiery yellow aspens reminded me of a glassmaker's forge. That landscape of high tilted plateaus and long vertical drops, of tawny meadows and patchy forests, was like nothing we had ever seen.

"What if we could live here for a year?" Steve asked.

His idea was to stay long enough to see the entire natural cycle from one autumn to the next. We would not be tourists passing through to someplace else but people who belong.

"And after a year?" I asked.

"Well, then we would move on to the next place and live there for a year," he responded.

He had it all planned out. A year isn't much time in the life of a place; to compensate, you would virtually live out–of–doors. In all weathers, there you would be (appropriately dressed, of course), binoculars looped around your neck, a field notebook tucked into your back pocket, waiting, watching, and waiting some more. You could try some of the classic naturalist techniques that we never seemed to have time for: hunkering down in a blind near a watering hole, sugaring for moths, calling for owls on moonlit nights. It would be an intensive immersion, like one of those language classes where you live, breathe, and speak nothing but Spanish for six weeks.

At the time, it sounded like a wonderful idea; now, newly sensitive to the importance of place in my life, I suspect that leaving at the end of the year would always be harder than we imagined.

Hearing a raven's rough call, I look up but do not see the bird. Snow dusts every ledge on the cliffs above me. I shiver inside my jacket. Too cold for comfort but not too cold for joy. How beautiful it is. Gray clouds wrap gray rocks until it is hard to tell where rocks end and clouds begin. Not–so–distant ridges float out of the mist, then disappear again. The edge of the world could lie a mile up the trail. Soon I will have to turn back, but for a moment I stand and stare. Time and time again, in one beautiful place after another, I have found myself wishing I belonged there. This time, I do. And if it seems too familiar at times, that is a small price to pay.

# 6

the brome among the poppies

Below us is Sabino Canyon on the left, Bear Canyon on the right, and between them Blackett Ridge is stretched out like a giant lying on his side. We are on his shoulder, an exhilarating perch. Twelve hundred feet below, the Phone Line Trail is a string draped across the landscape. Two mobile red dots on the string look like spider mites but are more likely hikers. White-throated swifts swish by our heads. A pair of turkey vultures floats by, first one, then a minute later, another. Their red heads droop and their long, black wings tilt from side to side as they ride the thermals, describing wide circles around our knoll with nary a wingbeat.

Down in the canyon bottom fourteen hundred feet below, cotton-woods and ashes are a bright and lively green. It's only March, and already they are fully leaved. Their winter vacation is a brief one in the desert, just a few months. Tiny people trundle up the road. Their voices drift up occasionally. Even if we shouted as loud as we could, they would not be able to hear us over the rush of water in Sabino Creek. Much of it is snowmelt from higher elevations—also a sign of spring.

Here on the ridgetop, butterflies have gathered to court and spar in the sun, yet another sign of spring: a few black swallowtails, a single red admiral, several painted ladies. The wings of the painted ladies, as they dash against one another, sound like the pages of a book fluttering in the wind.

If Steve and I stepped off the path, we would be shin-deep in wildflowers: lupine, wild hyacinth, desert chicory, popcorn flower, peppergrass, phacelia, wild carrot, fiddleneck, brittlebush, wild delphinium, desert dandelion, California poppy. The colors are yellow, white, and blue, mainly, with pink and purple and orange accents. Someone might have dumped all this color here with a shovel; it is mounded under paloverde trees and saguaros, heaped around boulders and rock piles. Talk about painted ladies! This is an astonishing transformation when your eyes are accustomed to the varied grays and muted greens of the desert in its Amish aspect. Hiking up the ridge, I listed seventy-four species of wildflowers in bloom right now, and there are doubtless others that I missed.

This is no more typical of the desert than snow. March arrives on a yearly basis but more often than not forgets to bring spring with it. Turning spring from a concept into a reality requires a lot of rain between October and February. The different kinds of wildflower seeds have different germination requirements—wet and cool, wet and cold, very wet yet not too cold, and so forth. If, as in most years, October comes and goes with no significant rainfall, we stop hoping for poppies and mariposa lilies in the spring. If November is also dry, we cross lupines off our wish lists. If rains finally start in December or January, the coldest months, we know that we can at least expect popcorn flower and fiddleneck. But if they delay until February, there will be few wildflowers at all. Nothing to say then but "maybe next year."

At our feet, a syrphid fly probes a wild hyacinth flower with its long tongue, searching for nectar. Its clear wings and pale, fuzzy body make it easy to mistake for a bee until it freezes in place with wings spread like a fighter jet. Wild hyacinths are lavender with small, tuliplike flowers. A dozen flowers in each cluster, three or four clusters on each plant, a thousand plants on this ridgetop: the arithmetic suggests that syrphid flies will not go hungry this spring. By May, plenty of seed will have set and fallen. The soil will hoard it for the next rainy winter, whenever that comes.

Growing up in southern California, I thought of spring as a literary phenomenon, something that happened mainly in books; willows sprouting furry buds, jack-in-the-pulpit poking up through snow, purple hepatica pushing aside brown leaves of beech and maple: the spring of Connecticut, perhaps, or eastern Pennsylvania. Sometimes in spring my parents, my sister, and I piled into the car with a picnic lunch and drove for hours across the desert to a place that had no name. When we got there, we saw long, slender hills awash with the colors of stained glass, like a rose window reflected across the landscape. Dazed with color, drunk with it, I wandered through vast fields of wildflowers, looking for as many kinds as possible. I could never resist picking the poppies even though I knew that their silky petals, as orange as persimmon flesh, would fall before the end of the day. This was not the spring I knew from books but some other phenomenon entirely, an extravaganza unnamed and unnameable except with the flowers themselves: tidy tips and filaree, owl's clover and farewell-to-spring, five-spot and Ithuriel's spear. After one of these excursions, I had a nightmare in which fields of lupines and poppies posed some kind of menace: the dream of a cautious, easily frightened child. A Jungian analyst might have seen archetypes in my dream: the dark side of beauty and innocence, the unperceived threat in the seemingly innocuous. "Too much excitement," my mother would have said.

A swallowtail circles my head, decides I am not in bloom, and flutters away to find something that is.

"Richard is calling this the best spring ever," I tell Steve.

And Ray and Jeanne came back from Baja California earlier this month, telling about sleeping in beds of lupines. A friend of a friend reported ajo lilies five to six feet tall on the sand dunes in northwestern Mexico. "From the knees down," she said, "my jeans were yellow with pollen."

Steve, poking among the rocks, announces, "Anemones, mostly in fruit, and *Thysanocarpus*, *Lesquerella*, and *Microseris*."

Ordinarily, I would be collecting now, too: plastic bags, field notebook, plant press, the usual routine. But somehow I cannot whip myself into a proper appreciation of the best spring in thirteen years.

"A good spring, but not a great one," I keep telling people who ask, and why do they query *me*, as if I were some grand old dame of botany at the age of forty-two?

Good springs are rare enough that I use them as chronological markers—the spring when I taught myself to identify plants, the spring when I worked at Organ Pipe Cactus National Monument, the spring when Steve and I fell in love. This year the marker is red brome, an annual grass with a Struuwelpeter head. The plants turn red-violet when the seeds ripen. There's more red brome than I would like this spring, more than I remember seeing in any other year. It belongs to the steppes of the eastern Mediterranean region. Seventy-five years ago only scattered patches of red brome grew in the Tucson area. Some had been deliberately planted by ranchers who were hoping to undo two years of drought and two decades of overgrazing. Even twenty years ago red brome was not especially common. Now it is everywhere, so much at home you might think it was a native plant.

Red brome is in many ways better adapted to the desert than the showy natives. It needs less rain to germinate and set seed. By emerging earlier than most of the native wildflowers, red brome preempts nutrients, water, and space that they could use. In a bad year, when native wildflowers are present only as seeds in the soil, red brome does well, and in a good year like this one it performs stupendously. Because it produces a bumper crop of seeds almost every year, the more red brome you have, the more you get. The sad corollary is that the more red brome you get, the fewer wildflowers you have.

If this particular spring is less spectacular than others, therefore, red brome is to blame. What's frustrating is that the good springs are so far apart, I can't remember how it used to be. I only know it was different. Not only different but better.


Looking up the canyon, we see the main ridge of the Santa Catalina Mountains, dark green splashed with white. We can pick out Mount Bigelow by the radio towers, and Mount Lemmon by the massive prow of Lemmon Rock, but the names of other peaks elude us. Singing from the outer branches of a nearby graythorn, a black-throated sparrow utters a pair of notes, a volley and a final tweedle–deedle-dee. When the shadow of a red-tailed hawk slides overhead, the sparrow falls silent. A female hummingbird hovers at the graceful wands of penstemon, dipping her bill into one pink flower after another.

Many land managers still advocate sowing exotic grasses on over-grazed ranges. They might well argue that my preference for native communities and unaltered habitats is a value judgment. Maybe it is; what I see around me, though, is the utter worthlessness of red brome. No caterpillars feed upon its foliage, no birds eat its minuscule seed. Red brome fills no role in the natural community, except that of spoiler. "Mediterraneanization," some call it, the replacement of native perennial grasses by red brome, wild oats, and other annual grasses from the Mediterranean region. The word is shorthand for the extirpation of a native plant community in a matter of decades.

If I were newly arrived from Michigan or Kansas, I would be thrilled with the desert this spring. But I have traded innocent pleasure for intimate knowledge. My childhood nightmare seems prophetic, now. The hidden menace was not the dark side of beauty but the brome among the poppies, the loss of wildflowers to weeds.

Loss of innocence always exacts a price. Barbara Tedlock, an American anthropologist, told how her Zuni Indian friends responded to the moon walk of 1969. In Zuni cosmology, the moon is the mother, as the sun is the father. When Neil Armstrong planted a flag in the Moon Mother's body and scooped out boxes of her flesh, devout Zuni worried that she would withdraw her gifts or, worse yet, inflict droughts, floods, extreme cold, and infertility. Others, especially the young men, questioned whether the Moon Mother truly was a deity.

Yet the Zuni adapted. A year or two later, Tedlock's friend Kwinsi had worked moon rockets and astronauts' helmets into a summer rain song that also included corn plants and alluvial silt. The song was written to accompany a dance. Tedlock concluded that "Zunis are indeed dancing, as they always have, in order to bring rain and fertility, but they are also dancing the modern world into place: giving it meaning, order, perhaps even a sacred existence."

Like human footprints on the moon, red brome cannot be undone. It is here to stay. Looking at this beautiful yet ruined spring, I wonder what song I can write, what dance I can perform, that will restore its order and meaning.

# 7

unblinkered eyes

"New Yorkers have Central Park, we have Sabino Canyon," a long-time resident of Tucson once told me, and he was right. Twenty years ago, when the road was still open to cars, you were lucky to find a place to park on any fine Saturday or Sunday in spring. Sabino Canyon was then a kind of urban enclave fingering into the wilderness. Now that trams ply the road at regular intervals, the crowds are somewhat reduced, but especially on sunny weekends in the spring, all the picnic areas are occupied well before noon, and every swimming hole is alive with shouting, dripping children.

Steve and I board the tram at the Forest Service visitors' center about a mile west of the canyon and settle in for the ride. Our fellow passengers seem evenly divided between pale Midwesterners with cameras and suntanned Tucsonans with ice chests and portable stereos.

Almost as soon as the tram enters Sabino Canyon, we are deep in the mountain's flanks. Here there is no gradual heightening of canyon walls. One moment we are heading for the canyon's wide mouth, the next inside a long, straight chute. Rooted in the Spanish word *caña*, for tube, and the Latin word *canna*, for reed, a canyon *should* be a deep channel with vertical or even incurving walls. Making your way up, down, or across one would be like scrambling around the interior of a giant cement pipe. My dictionary, subscribing to this view, defines *canyon* as "a narrow chasm with steep cliff walls" and illustrates it with a photograph of the Grand Canyon, which is like using a portrait of Shakespeare to convey the concept of *writer*. There are indeed steep cliff walls in Sabino Canyon, but they seem inserted more or less at random into the slopes, as are the tilted shelves of bedrock and isolated blocks of gneiss. This is a Cubist's idea of a canyon landscape, a Grand Canyon that has been shattered and shifted and stacked helter-skelter.

Our driver today is Al, a trim, middle-aged man with gold-rimmed glasses and a tanned face suffused with pink. He has the singsong voice native to tour guides everywhere, with odd stresses that depend more on meter than meaning. "The palo*verde is* the state *tree* of Arizo*na* and paloverde in *Span*ish *does* mean *green stick,*" he chants. His spiel, a mixture of fact and misinformation, reminds me of the way I picked up church hymns as a small child. "Christ the royal master leans against the phone," I sang out with equal parts of conviction and puzzlement. As the tram purrs up the road, Al tells us that the huge boulders in the canyon bottom fell from the walls in the earthquake of May 1887, which is correct, but then he says, "Sabino Canyon is a true desert oasis, which means that the leaves change color in the fall."

The road crosses the stream several times: in dry seasons, the roadbed makes a bridge across stagnant pools; in wet seasons, as now, it serves as a ford. This morning, an entire family is barefoot after wading over one bridge, and they're sitting at the edge of the roadway, putting their shoes back on. All three of the little boys have sticks. The smallest child, a half-naked girl, is running in circles, arms pointed straight up. Mud spatters her chest, a good sign. You can't participate in nature by remaining as clean as if you had just stepped out of the tub.

Al points out Thimble Peak, a nipple of rock on the canyon rim. I had forgotten—or never noticed—how the cliffs stand on the rim like the fur on an angry cat's back. All the rock here is gneiss: on high cliffs, it is rusty and streaked like bacon; along the stream it is bleached to pale gray or white. Al directs our attention to the Acropolis Cliffs, an immense tablature of zebra-striped rock some four hundred feet tall. Blackett Ridge lies on top; we can see the point from where, a month ago, we watched minuscule people file along this very road. Since then, spring seems to have tumbled down the ridge and spread along the canyon bottom. Sunny slopes are yellow with brittlebush, and ocotillos flame above our heads. A few early prickly pear cacti are in bloom with extravagant yellow flowers, extravagant both because they are large and because they last only a single day.

We itch to get off the tram and out into the spring, and when Al finally stops at the end of the road, we practically leap to the pavement. The return trip will begin in about eight minutes, Al announces; he will toot the horn when he is ready to leave. We slip into our packs. Evidently we are the only people heading up the trail. The other passengers are milling around the parking lot or standing listlessly, as if caught in an existential crisis. Everything in their posture and expression asks, Now what? They don't seem to understand that a small additional expenditure of effort would double their pleasure in the day and the place.

"They don't know what they're missing," I tell Steve, smug and self-satisfied until I realize the same charge could be leveled against us. We have hardly explored the wilderness above Sabino Basin, for instance. We do what we can. Maybe the people at the end of the road have gone as far as they can for now.


The trail stays well above the canyon bottom, climbing gently among saguaros and paloverdes. Below us, the stream curves around bouldery beaches where the rounded rocks are as big as basketballs, as white as bone. Across the way, a slender waterfall hangs from the edge of a cliff. Thin spouts of water shuffle downward, falling for a hundred feet or more into a coppery pool. Like the spring wildflowers, the falling water is a seasonal delight. In another month, only the pool will remain, and a month after that, a circle of papery, black organic matter will show where the water was.

There was a time when my automatic response to this scene would have been to whip out my camera and capture it on film. A revealing choice of words, "capture," as if the subject of the photograph were otherwise apt to escape, a real possibility with squirrel or deer but not much of a risk with a waterfall. My urgency at such moments revealed that what I wanted to capture *was* the moment—not only the landscape but the haunting warble of a hermit thrush secreted among the pines, the brisk little breeze running up the back of my neck, the rich organic fragrance of decaying leaves, the whirr of a hummingbird's wings, and perhaps the flash of blue as a Steller's jay bounced from branch to branch. The fact that I never consciously acknowledged this complex desire may have accounted for my disappointment when my pictures came back from the developer.

No disappointment today. No camera. When it was stolen six years ago, I was at first determined to replace it as soon as I could afford to do so. This took some time. Meanwhile, I found myself reaching for a nonexistent camera with decreasing frequency as the impulse to preserve a moment on film gave way to the impulse to experience it as fully as possible, as it unfolded. By the time I had saved enough money to buy another camera, I had lost the desire to have one.

A hummingbird zooms by our heads and perches on the topmost twig of a paloverde. Turning its head from side to side, it whistles— a high, thin sound with a falling inflection. As the sun catches the feathers on its head, I see a flash of purple. He must be a Costa's hummingbird, and the brilliant purple feathers are his gorget. More purple feathers poke out to either side on his neck, giving him the look of a fiercely mustachioed pirate.

As he moves, his entire head turns from purple to violet-blue to black. His iridescent feathers contain clear platelets that act like prisms. Sunlight, containing colors of every wavelength, passes freely into the platelets, but only certain wavelengths pass back out. Exactly which ones depends on platelet thickness. For the Costa's hummingbird, it is the shorter wavelengths, the blues and violets. For the rufous hummingbird, which has a brilliant orange or vermilion gorget, it is the longer wavelenths. The exact color varies according to the angle of illumination. If the sun is directly behind me, the Costa's gorget is purple. If it comes from the side, black seems the predominant color.

The Costa's swoops into the air, then hurtles toward a small catclaw. Stopping short of a collision, he hovers for a second, then zigzags back and forth, buzzing all the while. Lacking a camera, I scribble a few notes on a scrap of paper about his performance. Hummingbirds use their gorgets in courtship and territorial defense, flashing the feathers as they dive-bomb potential lovers and enemies. This hummingbird's dance is meant for a female Costa's, nearly invisible in the dense foliage. She sits unmoved through his entire sequence, then darts away to the shelter of a different shrub. She may be playing coy or genuinely seeking safety. In the hummingbird world, lovers and enemies are not necessarily well differentiated, and courtship is often brief and fierce.

Sometimes I think that the impulse to fling a camera in front of one's eyes is the same as the impulse that threw Saul to the ground on the road to Damascus; our instinct is to protect ourselves from the blinding presence of the sacred. Other times I think it is the only way we poor humans can find of participating in the lives of wild creatures. We can't drop to our knees and howl with the coyotes— well, we could but they aren't going to thank us for it—but we can try to get their searching gaze on film in the hope that afterwards it will remind us of what we felt, that ineffable shiver of sheer animal attraction mingled with awe, fear, and yearning. Sometimes I think that because they—coyotes, cougars, coatis—won't accept us on their terms, we capture them on ours. Or maybe the photographic impulse is even more primitive than that: we hope to capture the souls of wild animals, as if afraid that we have no souls of our own, only a hyperdeveloped cerebral cortex that sets us apart from the wild world.

Steve and I stop for lunch at Hutch's Pool, a giant shoe box with bedrock sides and bottom but no lid. It holds a perennial pool, a favorite swimming hole for those hardy enough to hike the four miles to get here. We are up for the hike but not for the water itself, which is quite cold. Instead, we sit side by side in the shade of a big rock, quiet, companionable.

Butterflies gather on the sand at a nearby seep—"mudding," this behavior is called. I count two tiger-tailed swallowtails and a half-dozen sulphurs, then inadvertently spoil the party by standing up. They scatter as they rise into the air. Within a few minutes, they reassemble and suck at the sand with simpleminded concentration, their tongues pumping liquid into their bodies. Their movements on the ground, a combination of flutter and drag, are clumsy and uncertain, as ungainly as a harbor seal on dry rock.

For fifteen, twenty, thirty minutes I watch them sit and suck, a short period in my life but a long one in theirs. They *could* be courting, mating, producing offspring—fulfilling the biological goal of every sexual organism. Instead, they concentrate on whatever mysterious substance the seep offers, perhaps some essential micronutrient, perhaps simply the moisture itself. Either way, its attractions are strong enough that even the normally pugnacious swallowtails sit within a wingbeat of one another.

We finish our lunch, and sling our packs onto our shoulders. "How many people do you think we'll see on the way back?" Steve asks. It's a guessing game he likes to play. One New Year's Day, he predicted we would see twenty-two hikers on our return trip to the car. That was way too many, I said, but refused to commit myself any further.

He kept track with growing dismay as the number quickly rose from twenty-two to one hundred twenty-two, an average of one person every minute. That day, the Santa Catalina Mountains seemed in danger of being loved to death.

Today, we pass only three or four hikers before we reach the road, a kind of miracle considering that tens of thousands of people visit Sabino Canyon every year. I wonder, not for the first time, how to turn more of these visitors into habitants. You can't blame people for wanting to escape the city on Saturday or Sunday; on the other hand, once they are here, they need to understand that Sabino Canyon is not an extension of their own backyards but a self-contained world that exists without reference to the city nearby.

For a while I worked on a project that involved matching historic landscape photographs. We worked in crews of three, usually, a photographer, a notetaker, and a photo interpreter. The procedure was to find the exact place where the original photographer stood and reoccupy it in every particular, facing the camera in the same direction, placing it at the same height, even, if possible, shooting at the same time of day and season. While the photographer fiddled with camera backs and film packs, the notetaker acted as scribe, recording camera speeds, f-stops, lenses, film types, and so forth; the interpreter, holding a copy of the historic photograph in her hands, compared it with the present-day landscape, assessing what had changed and what had remained the same. Interpreting change was usually my role. The task required a fierce concentration because I had to orient myself in two different scenes at once—on the photograph in my hands and on the landscape under my feet. Meanwhile, the photographer would be exercising an intense concentration of his own, figuring out settings and angles and heights, shifting the tripod forward or back, up or down, seeking to duplicate the original view as faithfully as possible. The entire process took at least thirty minutes, sometimes longer. At the end, the photographer would come out from under his dark cloth, blink in the bright sun, and ask me, "Well, what changes did you find? What happened here?" He had necessarily been so taken up with the technical details that he had had no opportunity to look at the scene. Or, rather, he had looked at it, but he had not seen it. That is the seductive power of a camera. It becomes a thing in itself instead of merely a useful tool.

When I think about how I was with a camera in my hands—darting from spot to spot to frame the best view, fiddling with settings and focus rings, sputtering because I had forgotten to cock the shutter and thereby missed the crucial moment—I see a person occupied with distracting herself, substituting ritual for attention. I see a person who was more interested in recording that something happened than in watching it as it happened. I see someone who had swallowed the lie promulgated by a culture of documentation, the lie being that memory alone is insufficient proof.

This is not a tirade against photography in general or photographers in particular. A number of my friends are professional photographers. I respect and value their work, but when I have a camera in my hands, I become blind to the world around me. When I pick up a notebook and a pen, on the other hand, my senses leap to attention. The act of writing works for me like a focus ring on a camera. But not for everyone: for my friend Doug, taking notes in the outdoors would be like banging pots and pans together at a symphony concert.

So, I am quite willing to believe that some people find that photography sharpens perception. Nevertheless, if Steve and I move away— or if we don't for that matter—would I trade my living memories of these mountains for photographs of them? I recall the time Steve and I saw a bear in the Santa Rita Mountains. We were halfway around the Bog Spring Trail and were sitting cross-legged on the ground eating lunch under some pine trees. Crackling noises from the bracken about fifty feet away, drew our attention to a large, brown animal, mostly hidden by foliage. A cow, we thought at first, but then it poked its head into a clearing and looked at us with the glittering eyes and pointed snout of a bear. Mutually hypnotized, we stared at it, and it stared at us. With eyes glued to the bear, Steve fumbled for his pack, trying with one hand to unzip the main compartment so he could fish out his camera. "Don't run away," he whispered to the bear and kept fumbling, fumbling, loath to remove his eyes long enough for an efficient search. The bear ambled away before Steve got his camera in hand. Too bad, but at least he kept the bear squarely in view for as long as he could. Life could escape you entirely if you were always reaching for a camera.

Back at the visitor center, yet another tram is filling up. Bicyclists and joggers stretch their leg muscles. Mothers sit beside their children on wide wooden benches. A big blue tour bus with tinted windows spills a group of elderly people into the parking lot. Mostly white-haired and plump, they filter slowly from the air conditioned bus into the warmth of the day. Some of them have cameras, which they focus on one another. Others do predictable things like walk up to saguaros and point.

I start to roll my eyes, then remember how, a few summers ago, I visited Zion National Park for the first time and watched as a family in a mini-van stopped at a numbered pull-out along the road. While everyone else waited in the van, the father jumped out and snapped a photograph of the designated attraction, then hopped back in and drove away. He never even turned the motor off.

At least these gentle visitors today are on their feet and off the bus. Maybe their next steps will take them toward the trail. You have to start somewhere, after all, and here is as good a place as any.

# 8

## living without walls

As I stand our three-legged backpacking stove on a level spot cleared of leaves, then line up the spoons, cups, and pans on a flat rock, I feel like I'm playing house. Except for the fact that I'm allowed to handle matches now, I could be about ready to turn out a fine batch of mud pies. Steve, meanwhile, arranges the bedroom in a clearing just big enough for our little tent, which is itself just big enough for two sleeping bags and two pairs of boots.

Many of the things we've brought on this three-day backpacking trip are miniaturized. The cheese grater is the size of a business card. The combination salt and pepper shaker is no larger than a spool of thread. Our flashlights tuck into the palms of our hands, as do our field notebooks. In comparison, our clothing—denim jeans, wool sweaters, flannel shirts—seems disproportionately heavy. Too bad we can't miniaturize it. Same for the eight water bottles, which weigh two pounds each when full. In southeastern Arizona reliable streams are few and far apart, and we plan our backpacking trips accordingly. Every day must start and end at a reliable water source. Getting from one source to another means carrying enough water for a full day. Our standard joke on these trips is the crying need for freeze–dried water.

We chose this spot for our camp because of the spring. Throughout most of its length, Sunnyside Canyon is dry. Here, where impermeable bedrock forces groundwater to the surface, a ribbon of water trickles among stones for fifty yards or so, then sinks back into the earth. Marsh plants—sedges, grasses, and spike–rushes—edge the stream, making a thick and wiry turf that rebounds underfoot. It is a pocket meadow, like the pocket gardens of London or Seattle. We call them *cienegas* here. Big Apache pines shed long needles that catch among the rushes, brown hachure marks on a green background. A few late violets nestle among the sedges. As tiny as it is, this meadow is too wide to leap, and when we walk on it, water seeps up and over the soles of our shoes.

Last month we wore shorts and tank tops for our hike up Sabino Canyon. Here, three thousand feet higher, we need sweaters and long pants. All afternoon, clouds have been thickening overhead, "as if someone poured starch on them," Steve says. We keep telling one another that it never rains in May. Steve is wearing his rain jacket anyway. Preventive magic.

Supper—spaghetti and meat sauce—won't take long to fix. I made the sauce at home a month ago from a pound of sweet Italian sausage, an onion, several cloves of garlic, three cans of tomato sauce, a can of tomato paste, and a teaspoon each of dried basil, oregano, and sugar. I simmered them together until the sauce was thick, then divided it between three cookie sheets, spreading the layers as thin as possible. I set the oven to its lowest temperature, put the cookie sheets inside and propped the door open with a wooden spoon. After four or five hours, most of the moisture had evaporated. The crumbly chunks that remained, while more reminiscent of dog kibbles than fine Italian cuisine, could be tightly sealed in plastic bags and kept in a cupboard for months. All I need do now is reconstitute the sauce using equal parts of water and kibbles, heat it thoroughly, boil the spaghetti, and grate a little Parmesan cheese into a bowl. I work more carefully in my wilderness kitchen than I do at home. Big, careless gestures that could spill a pot of simmering spaghetti sauce or upset a bowl of grated cheese are out of place when the food supply is strictly limited.

*Everything* is strictly limited. That is the essence of the game, like needing the ball to score in basketball or football. One trick is to make as many implements as possible do double duty: a cereal bowl can serve as a dinner plate, a pot lid as a frying pan, a folded sweater as a pillow; another is to make them tiny. See above. And still another is to live daringly and leave the extras at home. Don't bring extra spoons (but be sure not to lose the ones you've got). Don't bring extra gloves (but keep the ones you're wearing dry).

A backpacking trip betrays how much I live with day to day that I apparently do not need. The !Kung peoples of the Kalahari, hunter-gatherers who live (and live well) by killing game and gathering the tubers and fruits of wild plants, have no fixed abodes. Rather they roam an area of about two hundred fifty square miles. From camp to camp they carry nothing except their babies and their bows and arrows. The landscape supplies everything else they need: medicine, food, clothing, and shelter. They would be mightily amused at my pride in having reduced our load to the bare necessities: sixty pounds of goods we think we cannot live without during the next two days. No wonder I feel like I'm playing house: the kitchen, the tents, and the backpacks themselves are a little island of domesticity that we have brought into the wilderness, and no amount of paring down will change that fact.

I can never shed my house completely. In some inexplicable way it accompanies me everywhere I go. This is what it means to be domesticated, I suppose, and if I desire to be a wild thing, my very language suggests that I never will. The !Kung, whose vocabulary is extraordinarily rich in words for terrain and vegetation, can render in a word or two some complicated idea like "the small acacia thicket near the rise beside the baobab tree." They have many terms for the exterior landscape; I have many for the interior one: kitchen, parlor, hall, bedroom, nursery, library, study, scullery, pantry. Limited by vocabulary, I might not be able to discern the small rise by the baobab, but by the same token, a !Kung woman entering my house might not see the richness there: the various rooms assigned to sleeping, cooking, reading, writing, bathing; the different cupboards for plates and glasses, pans and small appliances, sheets and towels; the separate drawers for flatware, kitchen utensils, and household tools. Backpacking, I might seem to approach the portable culture of the !Kung, but really I have not. My house is more than walls: it is a point of view and a lifetime's worth of habits.

After washing the dishes, we settle by the creek to read. The water gurgles as it spills over the rocks. Nearby, a New Mexico locust droops under fragrant, pink flowers. A hummingbird makes one last visit to the blossoms; we glimpse her white eyebrow, then she is gone. A squirrel discovers us and squeaks and scolds from its hidden perch among the pine needles.

A few raindrops spot the pages of my book. "Rain on May 31st," Steve says in wonder. We have just enough time to cover our backpacks and zip ourselves into the tent before it begins in earnest. Raindrops drumming on the tent fly drown out the stream at first, then slacken to a whisper. The tent brightens and dims as clouds shift overhead.

The storm lasts until darkness falls. Then the only sounds are the occasional tap and slither of an oak leaf on the tent fly and the interrogative call of a whippoorwill. "Purr-purr-ill? Purr-purr-ill?" it cries, near then far. As its song winds around and around our tent, I drowse and waken, then drowse again. The canyon walls seem far away, the sky seems very close. Our little tent is a craft that could be afloat in any stretch of time or space, and we may awaken on Venus or in Oz.

---

The purity of first wakefulness: light suffuses the tent, our craft has landed. Outside, water ripples over stones, and a black–headed grosbeak sings his lilting song, slurred phrases so similar in intonation to human speech that I keep straining to hear the words.

After a quick breakfast of coffee, hot chocolate, and granola and powdered milk, we break camp. As we amble up the canyon bottom, sticking more to the stream bed than to the old road that serves as a trail, we stop often for a closer look at the little plants tucked among the stones and sedges. For two years now, we have been working on a flora—a complete plant list—of the Huachuca Mountains, and we don't want to miss anything.

I find a kind of pale yellow dandelion among the rushes: a characteristic cienega plant in southern Arizona, Steve says, not known from many locations, well worth collecting. On dry banks we find candytuft, Huachuca lupine, and pussytoes. We bicker amiably over a red–freckled monkeyflower: *Mimulus guttatus*, Steve says, *Mimulus nasutus*, according to me, and both of us know that if we cannot reach agreement, one or the other will have to collect and identify it, an unpleasant prospect since, as we know from experience, resolution will be no easier to achieve in the laboratory than in the field. Okay, *Mimulus guttatus*, I say. Taxonomy by consensus.

This canyon bottom forest, a mixture of evergreens, looks much the same year–round. A bird's–eye view would show a nearly solid blanket of green, mostly oaks of several different kinds. William James wrote a book about the varieties of religious experience; I could write one on the varieties of oak woodland, I think, and for a similar purpose: to rejoice in the infinitely diversified expression of a seemingly unified phenomenon. On the driest slopes, oak woodland is dwarfed and gnarled. Ancient trees, their trunks as thick as Steve's arm, grow only four feet high but spread to six. Such knee-high woodlands remind me of the black spruce thickets Thoreau found during his ascent of Mount Katahdin in Maine. So densely interwoven were their canopies, he could not walk between them; instead he walked on top, a philosopher on a forest. Our dwarf oak woodlands are not quite that dense; even so, they are tangled enough that the only way in or out is usually on one's knees.

Here, where soil is thicker and life is lived not quite so close to the bone, oaks grow tall enough to filter the sunlight. A walk in these sun-dappled woodlands is like being underwater. Woodland oaks grow crowded—there's no room for their canopies to spread—so their branches look coppiced, like trees pruned too often for fuel. Their trunks are knotted, leaning this way and that, yet there is always room to walk among them. Underneath, the leafy carpet is a mixture of browns: fawn, mahogany, copper, sienna, umber, taupe.

Although we loosely call them evergreen, these oaks drop and renew their leaves in late spring. Then, within a month or so, the oak woodland looks first scorched, then verdant. The new leaves are soft and vulnerable at first, but they quickly harden, becoming leathery and sharply pointed and thick-skinned, a leaf for all seasons. An ecologist would call them sclerophylls, which means hard-leaved. A poet would note their pinched and stingy nature, well suited to a parsimonious environment where annual rainfall seldom exceeds twenty inches and the two rainy seasons—winter and summer—are separated by months of drought.

A flock of gray-breasted jays leapfrogs ahead of us, calling in raucous voices. These are big, bold birds, dusty blue above, dingy white beneath. "Wheet, wheet," they shout, and their wings clap the air like horses' hooves. No hope of sneaking up on squirrel or deer or bear once jays have discovered you. When we finally pass out of their territory, they fall behind and silence enfolds us like a glove.


The road becomes a footpath thickly sifted over with fallen leaves. Steve finds a hummingbird's nest on the ground and hands it to me, saying, "Because it's made of lichens, you could say it's still alive." The nest, a perfect hemisphere made of fine grass stems interwoven with soft, woolly lichens, would fit inside a demitasse cup. For a split second, I am afraid that Steve wants it for himself. But he means for me to have it and provides a plastic box so it won't get crushed.

He already knows that when I want these things, I want them ferociously. Anything too large or too lively to be carried home—a slab of limestone, a garter snake—becomes a source of piercing regret for hours or even days. He himself brings home few keepsakes: one time a handful of coffee bean shells from a beach in Baja California, another time a piece of lava from a Hawaiian volcano. And when I ask him what he wants—for Christmas or birthdays or anniversaries—he is apt to say, "Peace in our time. Extraordinary experiences in nature. A national championship for the Arizona Wildcats." Nothing that can be wrapped up and put in a box.

A long, steady, uphill pull brings us to the crest of the Huachuca Mountains by lunchtime. I spread out the ground cloth and, with some pride, array our meal upon it: pumpkin bread, cream cheese, Ritz crackers, peanut butter, fruit leather, dried bananas, teriyaki beef jerky, lemonade. The pumpkin bread, fruit leather, beef jerky, and dried bananas are from my own kitchen; the rest is from the grocery store. Plastic is what makes this feast possible: plastic bags, plastic wrap, plastic jars, plastic bottles, plastic knives. Seeking a closer connection to the natural world, we come equipped with five or six types of plastic. The irony, an uncomfortable one, reminds me once again of the !Kung, whose relationship with nature is one of confident dependence. How different it is for modern–day backpackers, who are urged *not* to live off the land, *not* to build shelters of natural materials, *not* to consume any resource but water, sun, and maybe wood.

Now that we are sitting still, gusts of wind chill our bones. It may be summer down in the desert, but it is barely spring at 8,300 feet. Only the earliest plants are in bloom: *Senecio wootonii*, thimble–shaped, yellow flowers on tufted stalks, and *Carex geophila*, the world's most common, least–collected sedge. A swirl of short, wiry leaves, *Carex geophila* resembles nothing so much as a grass that has yet to bloom, and even good botanists pass it without a second glance.

We collect both the *Carex* and the *Senecio*, one or two plants of each, roots and all, tucking them in small plastic bags. The weather is cool, so our specimens should last until tomorrow when we return to the truck and the plant press. Eventually, these two specimens, like everything else we collect, will be deposited at the university herbarium, a kind of library for pressed plants.

The ridgetop trail turns into a ridgetop firebreak, my least favorite kind of walking. A good trail is ergonomically designed, fitted to the capacities of human legs and lungs. A good road, while designed for vehicles and not nearly as pretty as a trail, is certainly not beyond the capacity of most walkers. But a firebreak, designed for neither, is an ergonomic disaster. In the Huachuca Mountains, firebreaks are steep and loose and rocky, tiring to hike up, treacherous to hike down. Several miles of firebreak leave us irritable and exhausted. "Whose idea was this, anyway?" Steve asks as we trudge up a hill so steep and loose that even a Jeep might have difficulty. *Our* wheels are spinning, anyway, and we are relieved when the firebreak joins the rutted dirt road in the bottom of Scotia Canyon.

Late in the afternoon we arrive at Peterson Ranch, a reliable water source. Long abandoned, this old homestead is in ruins, and nothing is left but a tumbledown shack and several cattle ponds engorged with rushes and cattails. We make camp on a terrace above the smallest of the ponds. From here we have a fine view of the densely wooded basin to the south and the forested ridge beyond, a green sweep of hill and hollow darkened here and there by cloud shadows. There is no one around for miles and miles.

"Women have no wilderness in them," Louise Bogan wrote. Right now, I might agree. This is a lovely place to camp, but it would be a lonely place to live if you needed more company than jays, ravens, a passing coyote, and an occasional bear.

After supper, we sit by a small campfire of juniper and oak, an atavistic pleasure—yellow flames, red embers, and orange sparks shooting into the darkness. Our campfires are rare enough that some stand out in memory. After a wet day in the Gila Wilderness, stars poked through the clouds, and our campfire, made from damp spruce, sent up sheets of smoke. On a cold and starry night in the

Sheep Range, we built a hot fire of juniper wood. The night was so cold and the fire so hot that it was a pleasure to walk away, chill off, then return to the permeating heat and the smell of incense. Jacques Lizot writes that among the Yanomami of the Venezuelan rain forest, "fire is a living domestic element; its abiding presence is almost human." Yanomami babies hardly leave their mothers' sides until the age of weaning. Then the family fire takes the place of a mother's bodily warmth. Fire is their home.

The fragrance of campfire smoke lingers on my sweater the next morning. After breakfast, we poke around the remnants of the old ranch house, a one-room cabin partly dug into a hillslope. The back wall of the cabin, lined with rocks and mortar, still stands, but the front wall is completely gone and the side walls are in disrepair. The floor, a concrete slab, is cracked and littered with leaves, twigs, and shreds of fabric.

"They must have led hard lives," Steve says. "A lot of hard work, ranching out here."

Then I realize that if not for these walls, this lingering human presence, I would not find the Peterson Ranch such a lonely place. To build walls is to construct a fortress against the wild. In West African hamlets, the villagers (especially the women) avoid the bush, the region beyond their cultivated fields. That's where demons live, and every villager knows of someone who went into the bush and came back insane or died a lingering death because of what was seen there.

"We tend," writes Nancy Mairs, "to ascribe to the other those qualities we prefer not to associate with our selves: it is the hidden, the dark, the secret, the shameful." If the indoors represents safety, self, the known, light, ego, and vested interest, the outdoors stands for danger, other, the unknown, shadow, id, and economic threat. Without walls to protect us, how can we remain self-contained? What is to keep us from dissolving into birds, trees, flowers, clouds, or stones?

Without walls, we would be like the dog Steve and I saw last summer on the other side of the range. Our campsite was within the National Forest but fairly close to a ranch, and as we sat talking in the dusk, I felt I was being watched and turned to look. There, staring at us from twenty feet away, was a young German shepherd, a red bandana around his neck, ears pricked up. When we greeted him, he scampered away and disappeared among the oaks. "Ranch dog," Steve said. I admired the facility with which he could pass back and forth between the tame and the wild: entering freely into the lives of his owners on the ranch yet becoming like a wild thing as he leaves the ranch behind and lopes across pastures and snuffles through woods.

We take down the tent, fold up the ground cloth, tuck dishes, stove, matches, and flashlights into their appointed places. The spot that was our camp looks strangely empty, although we occupied it for only one night. Remembering that ranch dog, I envy his ability to inhabit two worlds without faltering. I am an animal as he is an animal, yet I am too little an animal to live in the wild. I live in the tame and visit the wild and never forget the difference between the two.

encumbered  9

Cicadas clatter from the oaks like a thousand wooden pencils knocking together. It's June and it's hot. Only ten or twenty minutes in the sun, and already my skin is red, flaming. June is our hottest and driest month, and the Parry agaves, blooming now in Scotia Canyon, are an emblem of the season. The leaves look burned or stripped of color—some bleached, some blackened, as though a maniac had strolled through the woods with a flame-thrower. The flower stalks have sucked the leaves dry, requisitioned every drop of moisture, every dot of sugar. There is nothing left for another season of bloom. Now they will die.

A dozen ravens circle continuously overhead, raking the air with rough caws, taking in the entire Scotia Canyon watershed as they sweep in great arcs. They cover acres with only a few wingbeats, sailing over the same terrain that Steve and I traversed so slowly and painfully last month. An inordinate number of raven feathers grace the ground as if the birds' intention is to fly around and around until all their feathers fall out. I pick one up. It is a full foot long, blue-black, and has a sheen like oily water. With some difficulty I pin it to my pack. Another memento.

Like the hummingbird nest, it will end up in a basket or a jar along with other keepsakes from the wild—a coyote skull, a rough chunk of agate, a dozen sand dollars, enough deer antlers to reconstruct an entire herd. I'm not sure why I bother, since at home I seldom sort through my basket of natural objects. Evidently the wanting, not the having, is the point.

Steve decides to collect on the ridge while I stroll up the narrow, spring-fed stream. Damselflies by the dozen dart ahead of me. At any given moment, at least three or four different kinds are visible. The tiniest, less than an inch long, has bright green eyes. Its body is so slender and translucent that it appears to be little more than two dots of phosphorescent paint somehow linked in tandem. Of course I want to know its Latin name, but economic realities make it unlikely that a fully illustrated guide to the damselflies of Arizona will ever appear in print.

Crouching beside the stream to collect a specimen of watercress, I catch a furtive underwater movement out of the corner of my eye, a dark, oval shape that is here, then gone. A giant water bug: I'm certain of it. My attention is riveted. I have wanted to see one ever since reading *Pilgrim at Tinker Creek,* in which Annie Dillard tells of watching a frog crumple before her very eyes, the victim of a giant water bug. I stir up the watercress, hoping to make the bug, or whatever it was, reappear. It doesn't. Instead, a few water striders dart away from me, and some whirligig beetles, vigilantly paranoid, triple their rate of spin. Back swimmers rise and fall in the water column. Tiny black beetles roll around like ball bearings. Caddisfly larvae in oak leaf cases inch across the sand.

Twenty years ago I would have noticed none of this. I yearned to be a naturalist but wasn't certain how to go about it. Sometimes I sat on a flat rock in the middle of a certain small creek. Hugging my knees to my chest, watching the water flow around me, I tried to think appropriate thoughts about nature and life, but my knowledge was too scant to serve as a hook for my attention, and soon my thoughts would spin far away. There was a secret to being a naturalist, I was certain, but I hadn't yet been able to discover what it was.

It wasn't so much a lack of patience—I've always been short on that—as it was a lack of guidance. Nature itself seemed chaotic, uninformative. I preferred natural history books, where the author provided structure and interpretation. Eventually, I stumbled onto a workable method, that of perusing field guides at home, then looking out-of-doors for whatever I had read about. I began to peer into streams as though money were glued to the bottom. Once I knew that back swimmers and water boatmen and caddisfly larvae existed, I saw them everywhere, but never once did I see a giant water bug. Until this moment. Maybe.

Annie Dillard's giant water bug may have been *Belostoma fluminea*. In Arizona I am more likely to encounter *Abedus herberti*. Both species are voracious predators; besides adult frogs, they feed on insects, tadpoles, and small fish. A giant water bug's forelegs are adapted for grasping, its jaws for piercing and sucking. As it bites, it injects enzymes that turn the internal tissues of its prey to soup. According to the books, giant water bugs can inflict a painful bite on humans; presumably, they inject too little enzyme actually to dissolve your bones.

To anyone not already enamored of insects, these habits hardly make a strong recommendation for closer acquaintance. None of it is abnormal behavior, though. It's simply ordinary insect business carried out on a scale that gets our attention. What appeals to me about giant water bugs is that the female lays her eggs on the male's back; he is then said to be "encumbered." (Any woman who has been pregnant will recognize the utter appropriateness of the term.)

I watch two back swimmers tussle. One flips the other, which rights itself so quickly all I see is a flash of silver. When righted, it is of course upside down according to my way of thinking. Its coloring is reversed, too. Instead of being dark on the back and light on the abdomen, like most animals, back swimmers are the opposite. To a predator peering down from above, the dark abdomen makes a back swimmer less visible against the stream bottom, while to a predator peering up from below, the light back blends with the silvery tones of water and sky.

A large insect slips out from under a stream bed rock and scurries back. My heart leaps, then sinks. With its pebbly back, the insect looked more like a toad bug than a giant water bug. But if it *was* a toad bug, it should be hopping at the water's edge, not sidling underwater. I tap on the rock, hoping to dislodge the bug. It stays stubbornly hidden. I poke a stick under the rock but stir up only clouds of sediment. Finally, I fumble in my pack for the plastic box that holds an Ace bandage and a few other necessities, and empty it out. One chance is all I will get, so I had better do it right. With a quick, unbroken movement, I dip the box into the water and scrape it against the rock. When I bring the box back up, it is overflowing, and a giant water bug is turning around and around in the swirling current inside.

It seems unlikely that something so fiercely desired could be so easily captured. Yet a giant water bug is indisputably what it is. And now I see that its back looks pebbly because it is covered with eggs. At this moment, I have nothing left to desire in life: not only have I a giant water bug but an encumbered male at that.

The bug swims in circles for a minute, then crouches on the bottom, pincer legs clasped over his head like a child in a civil defense drill. Vaguely shield-shaped and about the size of a half-dollar, he is dark brown all over except for the peg-shaped eggs, which are pale gray with light brown tips. They stand on end like bowling pins, packed side by side over his entire back. Without his care, few would hatch normally. Not that he does much more than occasionally rock up and down in moving water, thereby keeping the eggs aerated and fungus-free. But male care of offspring is rare enough in the animal kingdom that even a modest effort in that direction arouses our interest.

Some turn-of-the-century entomologists responded indignantly to the phenomenon of a male literally burdened with offspring. "Enforced servitude," one of them called it. Another claimed that "the male chafes under the burden." To a slight extent, they were right; there *are* disadvantages for the male giant water bug. When encumbered, he is three times heavier than normal, which exacts a price in agility and speed, making him more vulnerable to predators and plastic boxes. I suspect, however, that these earlier entomologists were less distressed at the male's plight than they were incensed at the female's irresponsibility. What kind of mother deposits her children with her mate and blithely departs forever?

Now entomologists have a different perspective. If most of the eggs that the male carries are his descendants—and it appears that they are—he has a stake in their success and will give them the best care despite increased risks. His stake is not emotional, of course, it is genetic, since the individual that contributes the largest number of genes to the gene pool is considered the most fit in evolutionary terms. Yet, watching my giant water bug swim around in his container, I can't help thinking about the absent female. Most insect mothers depart forever after laying their eggs—that's nothing unusual. But the female giant water bug has somehow finagled the male into bucking an evolutionary trend stretching back millions of years, and that earns my admiration and envy.

It is not hard to imagine how it might have come about. Most insect eggs suffer a high predation rate because they are placed on a stem, leaf, or rock with camouflage as their only defense. Eggs of aquatic insects encounter additional hazards, from burial by floodwater deposits to scour by strong currents. The female giant water bug has found a perfect if somewhat *ad hoc* solution: the broad back of her mate, which is resistant to currents, predators, and shifting substrates and better yet, otherwise unemployed.

Steve returns, and for the first time today I remember with a pang that we might be moving, probably to a place where there are no giant water bugs. He says, "I hope you weren't bored, waiting so long." He has been gone an hour, he says. It seems like ten or fifteen minutes.

He duly inspects the giant water bug, which is still hunkered down on the floor of the box. "What are you going to do with it?" he asks, perhaps remembering another occasion when a few tadpoles, too fiercely desired to be left behind, made the long drive home in a mayonnaise jar, and none survived the trip. *I* remember it, anyway, and reluctantly, I empty the box into the water.

Steve and I amble downstream together. In a bedrock pool the size of a punch bowl, four giant water bugs are milling around. I am astonished at how common they are. How is it that I never noticed them until today? They rise to the surface to get oxygen, tilt back down to the bottom, fumble with their fierce pincers in the sediments, hunting but not finding. One grabs at a tiny water beetle, then lets it go. They ignore the water striders and back swimmers altogether. Perhaps what they want is tadpoles. Possibly they've already depleted this little pool of that particular delicacy.

The creek is awash in long strands of algae that drift in the water like hair. Every time I lift some with a stick, I find another giant water bug. By the time we walk fifty feet, I have found a half dozen or more. Some are encumbered, some not. Judging by the numbers, male care of offspring can work pretty well.

# 10 still hunting

Early on summer mornings, especially after a rainy night, a thin mist sometimes hangs over Hospital Flat, a long, tilted meadow high in the Pinaleño Mountains. The mist emanates from the little creek, not much wider than a man's hand, that slips down the center. The creek banks are so thick with grasses and sedges that you cannot see the water until you have stepped in it. This morning, the meadow is wet with dew, and the air is so humid that my clothes feel damp to the touch. On this hygroscopic morning, I feel as well as know why the meadow is so lush, the encircling forest so dense.

I pull my jacket more tightly around me and think the thoughts I think whenever my mind is not more urgently occupied these days—thoughts about leaving and loss. But why, asks the little voice who sits at the back of my mind, contradicting 50 percent of my mental utterance, why do you always cast your not-so-imminent departure in terms of loss? Surely there are gains to be made as well.

Think, for example, how many of the writers associated with one particular place actually wrote about that place when they were far removed from it. When Ernest Hemingway wrote about coming of age in Michigan, he was living as an expatriate in Paris. When Edward Abbey wrote about the canyon lands of Utah in a manuscript that later became known as *Desert Solitaire,* he was living, I believe, in New York City. Same for Willa Cather when she recreated the Midwestern prairies where she had spent her childhood. If she had not been willing to move, we probably would not have *My Antonia.*

Once the mist burns off and the entire meadow is bathed in sun, thousands of insects materialize from wherever they spent the damp and chilly night. Some, like these six bumblebees packed together on a lavender thistle, have materialized too soon. In the shade, the temperature is around fifty degrees Fahrenheit, too cold for bumblebee flight. To perform tasks such as gathering nectar, a worker bumblebee must first warm up to a temperature of about one hundred degrees. It does so partly by behavior, such as basking in the sun, and partly by physiological means, such as pumping its abdominal muscles to generate heat. God knows how these bees got here, because until sunlight brings warmth to the thistle, they are incapable of getting away.

They can move, however; in extremely slow motion they dip their tongues in and out of the thistle florets like drilling rigs. Leaning close, I cup the thistle head in my hand, exhale warm breath onto the bees. As if by magic, they stir their legs and shudder their wings and start to clamber about.

Hemingway in *A Movable Feast* sagely noted that sometimes people, like other growing things, require transplanting. You move a potted plant from one container to another when it becomes pot-bound, when its roots are crowded into a tiny volume of soil. In a larger pot, the roots have more soil from which to extract water and nutrients. The entire plant benefits, and after a period of adjustment grows by leaps and bounds. In the case of creative writers, transplantation seems to free the imagination, giving it the leeway it needs to recombine events and people and places in ways that never happened in real life but seem perfectly true when you read them.

The benefits for scientists are not quite so clear. To a chemist, one well-equipped laboratory must be much like another, and it makes little difference in terms of experimentation whether it is in Tucson or Timbuktu. Location does matter to a biologist. Almost the first question I ask when someone describes a plant, hoping I can identify it sight unseen, is "Where did you find it?" Except for a few so-called cosmopolitan species that occur around the world, plants and animals are restricted in distribution to particular regions and within those regions to particular habitats. Biology is 80 percent location, and a dislocated biologist is almost by definition either painfully disoriented or virtually overwhelmed by new stimuli.

As I stroll across the meadow, successive waves of grasshoppers leap away from my advancing legs like blades of grass flying from the whirling blades of a push lawn mower. Some make a ratcheting sound like a stick dragged along a picket fence. Others sputter like loosed balloons or buzz like power saws. Large, shiny, black flies scramble across yellow thistles with comical frenzy, a bunch of White Rabbits late for important dates. Painted ladies, by far the most common butterfly, nectar on the bountiful yellow flowers of sneezeweed, one butterfly per flower. Fritillaries, the second most common butterfly, seek out the hawkweeds: big, orange butterflies teetering on tiny, orange flowers. Butterflies, like bees, depend partly on air temperature to keep their bodies mobile. As a cloud passes across the sun, the fritillaries freeze in place, wings spread. When sunshine returns, they become animated again, pirouetting on flower heads and pumping their wings.


In the days of the Indian wars, soldiers from Fort Grant at the base of the Pinaleño Mountains were transported to Hospital Flat for treatment and rest. Their big tents must have skirted the meadow the same way as do the tents of modern campers today. I am not ill or wounded, but for a moment I almost wish I were so that I could stay here forever to recuperate.

In any case, I can stay for a while. Sitting, I sink from view into a streaky canvas of green and blue and yellow and pink and white. So much texture in a meadow. I had never realized. Wiry stems of grass and sedge crisscross every which way, as numerous as broomstraws. You could hardly fit a broomstraw in among them, you would think, except that thousands of wildflowers have somehow managed to squeeze themselves in—Saint-John's-wort, gentian, harebell, shooting star, lady's tresses, and nodding onion. The onion inflorescence is a dozen umbrella spokes, each tipped with a single bell-like flower. Stamens and pistil dangle from the pink bells like clappers. As I watch, a small, wasplike fly hangs from one clapper and gathers pollen from the anthers.

There must be a hundred different plant species in this meadow. With one or two exceptions, they are perennials, plants that come back year after year from underground roots or stems. Many, especially the grasslike sedges and rushes, are rhizomatous: their underground parts are long, horizontal stems with leafy shoots at frequent intervals. Rhizomatousness is a rapid way to find and occupy pinholes of space, much faster than starting a seed in the same spot. At the edge of the meadow, seedling ponderosa pines make a wobbly start among dry grasses. The Forest Service, to preserve the meadow, will cut them in due time. In the middle of the meadow, where I am, the sward is so thick that pine seeds drifting onto it would never touch bare dirt. Seeds of meadow wildflowers probably stand their best chance on the mounds of dirt grubbed up by gophers.


This is what I like best: to walk someplace and sit. Steve and I are always moving through the landscape. We should stay in one place more often and let the landscape move through us. The meadow flows around me, green and moist and alive. A bee hovers at my knee, trying to decide if the blue of my jeans represents a genuine flower or a tiresome fake. I remember *Through the Looking Glass*, in which Alice overhears a conversation between a rose and a tiger lily. "If only her petals curled up a little more," says the lily of Alice's skirt, "she'd be all right."

At the meadow's edge, a hairy woodpecker hammers at the trunk of a ponderosa pine. Bark flies into the air like wood curling from the teeth of a power saw. The woodpecker seems unaware of me, and I like that; too often my experiences in nature are of the backs of animals running away from me.

My best moments out-of-doors seldom happen when I am questing. They drop over me when I am a quiet receptacle. The time we stood beneath a barn owl as it rose through a narrow cleft in the rocks and out into the blue sky; the time we watched a hummingbird feed her single nestling; the time we heard a hundred elks bawling and singing at dusk—these are the moments I remember, yet I was searching for none of them at the time. I was simply being, and doing so quietly. "Still hunting" is Joseph Cornell's excellent term for it.

Last week, cleaning the kitchen, I found a small black bug underneath the drainboard. It lay on its back with legs folded, apparently dead. I brushed it toward the floor with my fingertips but instead of dropping off the counter, it somersaulted into the air with a faint click and landed upright. I poked it again. Another click and flip. It was a click beetle, of course, the first I had ever seen. The click beetle can snap a small lobe on its underside into a matching depression; unsnapping the lobe makes it recoil into the air.

When I told my friend Tony that I had seen my first click beetle, he was incredulous.

"*How* old are you?" he asked. He could not believe that I had lived forty-odd years in such abysmal ignorance. "They're not at all uncommon in oak woodland," he said.

I pointed out that I do not usually search for insects; my tendency is to let them come to me. Perhaps nature-watchers, like lizards, could be categorized according to feeding strategy. Some lizards sit and wait for insects or other edible morsels to amble by, like the horned lizard in my backyard who plops himself down near an ant trail and snaps up the occasional ant. Others pursue their prey with vigor and a modicum of reptile cunning, like the Yarrow's spiny lizard that leaps on beeflies as they bask on sunny rocks. So it is with naturalists. While some pursue nature with checkbook and passport, trotting off to Antarctica or Africa with visions of penguins or pangolins dancing in their heads, others choose a nearby spot—maybe as close as their own gardens—and seat themselves comfortably, aware that they may have a long wait.

Either way, the more time you spend out-of-doors, the more you will see. This is mainly a matter of statistics and probability. Spend enough time in a supermarket parking lot, and you can hardly help seeing pigeons mate on telephone wires. Spend enough time in the desert, and sooner or later you are bound to see a roadrunner catch a lizard.

The more often you intersect the time and place of some vivid, unforgettable incident, the more observant you become. Years ago I wrote a story that required a cattle tank, a watering hole made by damming a shallow drainage. Runoff collects after heavy storms and often remains many months, making a reliable place for range cattle to find water. In my story, two characters named Jem and Holly stop beside a watering hole in the desert. Jem, a man of few words, says, "Cattle tank. The Indians call them *charcos*." Holly notices that a clump of cattails emerges from the water and that the mud around the tank is roughened by hoofprints of cows. Then they leave.

Several years after I wrote this brief scene I crouched beside a real cattle tank. Tangled strands of pondweed fringed the pond. Tiny aquarium snails clung to the stems. Separating the pondweed with my hands, I discovered two nearly translucent insects that looked like underwater walkingsticks. I brought my hand under one and lifted it toward the surface for a better look. Its legs were like threads, and two frilly appendages fluttered on its back. Later, I learned that it was a water scorpion, a carnivore with piercing mouthparts that waits until an insect or tadpole happens along. Their beaks, I read, are capable of piercing human skin.

I could have been hurt, but I wasn't. I was enchanted. Back swimmers appeared at the surface, then slid back down into the murky water. Electric blue damselflies tacked across the pond. Mud at the perimeter had preserved the deep footprints of deer, coyote, and human. Hundreds of bees and wasps hovered over the mud, touching down briefly for sips of water. My fictional cattle tank, I realized with shame and shock, had been lifeless and inert, bearing as much resemblance to the real thing as a wish for a child resembles the rich and gritty reality of genuine parenthood.

The more observant you become, the more your scope of interest widens. Incidents you might have overlooked in the past now catch your attention—a bee at your jeans, a beetle under the drainboard, a translucent insect at the edge of a pond. Joseph Cornell asks, "Can we really *expect* to experience one of those 'rare moments' every time we go out into nature? That's not as unreasonable as it may sound, for nature is *full* of those rare moments. The only thing that prevents us from being aware of them is our own frame of mind."

Many times out-of-doors, it seems to me that nothing is happening. To amuse myself, I do then what I am doing now: I inspect the ground or the tree trunks or the rocks. I am often amazed at what I find. Once I poked apart some coarsely hairy scat on a trail in the Pinaleño Mountains. It contained two cartilaginous objects which, I informed Steve, had to be the claw sheaths of a mountain lion. Afterwards, a wildlife biologist told me that they were in reality fawn hooves. "Probably a black bear stumbled across a newborn fawn and ate it on the spot," he said. A different time, my friend Betsy found a mouse tail on the pavement outside our office—no blood or innards, only the silky tail, black above and white below. And then there was the time I found my first bagworm, but that's another story. As Joseph Cornell pointed out, there is always something to see out there. The unpredictable variable is ourselves.

We bring who we are to the understanding and interpretation of any experience, and we make the experience as it makes us. I remember how at church camp many years ago we children would go our separate ways for fifteen minutes every morning to "meditate." I sat on a sunny boulder in the pines with my Bible in my hands and waited for something to happen to me. Nothing did—no visitations of spirits or angels, no intimations of immortality. I was simply a girl on a rock, a little bored, a little impatient. If I had known then what I know now, I would have been digging in the pine needles at my feet or pulling apart a loose piece of bark. Searching for meaning in all the right places, I would have found more than enough to occupy a quarter hour of my life.

Mount Graham
*Pinaleño Mountains*

# 11

a broken mountaintop

High in the Pinaleño Mountains, the silence is as deep as the forest is tall. It fills space, like light; occupies time, like words. A jet passes high overhead, parting the stillness for a few moments. Then silence rolls in like water. The trail underfoot is quiet, too, soft from accumulated fir needles and bark, all damp and rotting together. *Duff* is the forester's term for it, a soft word as is the thing it connotes. Moss paints the duff with Kelly green stripes. Each stripe denotes a fallen log, now disintegrated. The forest floor must be thousands of trees deep by now, like Jerusalem, one ancient city built upon another, the modern town still thriving on the surface.

From the outside, the forest seems a wall. Inside, it is more like a loosely woven basket, dim but airy and remarkably spacious. Blue sky shows between the basket weave of spruce and fir, and there is not a breath of wind. Only silence, and trees as dark as a green bottle filled with red wine. Tasha Tudor, an illustrator of children's books, said, "Supposing you only saw the stars once every year. Think what you would think, the wonder of it." These days I can't help adding a doleful corollary: supposing we moved, and I were never to see this again.

When the trail spills us into a sunny clearing, we stop for the sheer pleasure of being in this space. Waist-high grasses and nodding blue harebells overhang the path. Thousands of mountain sunflowers as yellow as corn mingle with the grasses and with pink thistles as stiff as military hairbrushes. It is Hospital Flat crowded into a teacup.

Atlantis fritillaries, orange butterflies inscribed with runic black markings, revel among the thistles. They reach their southern limit here in the Pinaleño Mountains, even though the Chiricahua Mountains some sixty miles to the south are nearly as high and just as wet. Engelmann spruce and long-tailed voles also go no farther south. It works the other way, too: the Apache fox squirrel, the Mexican long-tongued bat, the Mexican chickadee, and many other birds and animals are found no farther north than the Chiricahua Mountains. The Pinaleño Mountains are unique in southeastern Arizona: not only the highest range, but also the only one where winters mimic in severity and length the winters of the Rocky Mountains to the north. For plants and animals, the Pinaleños represent a kind of biological escarpment between the Rocky Mountains and the Mexican highlands, a Maginot Line between northern and southern forms.

As the trail leads back into the forest, Steve points at a small, delicate squirrel running along the top of a log. When it runs through a bar of sunlight, we see the ruff of silver around its fluffy tail. The squirrel carries a big purple mushroom in its mouth like a dog with a frisbee. It hops from the log to the trunk of a cork-bark fir, then with perfect grace shins up the tree, still clenching the mushroom. It runs out on a limb and wedges the fungus into a forked branch, tucking it down well among the lichens. Then the squirrel runs down the far side of the tree and disappears. I wait a long time but do not see it again.

Squirrel sign is more plentiful than squirrels: protracted trills from high overhead, freshly cut spruce cones scattered across the ground, and middens under certain trees. These are Mount Graham red squirrels, an endangered subspecies of *Tamiasciurus hudsonicus*, variously known as the red squirrel, the spruce squirrel, the pine squirrel, and the chickaree. In parts of their range, red squirrels are so numerous that they are considered a nuisance. On Mount Graham, they hardly constitute a presence, much less a nuisance. As a result of logging and competition from the introduced Abert's squirrel, the population has dwindled to about one hundred fifty animals. Like the Atlantis fritillary and the Engelmann spruce, this is as far south as red squirrels go in Arizona. The nearest populations are in the White Mountains nearly one hundred miles north. In the Pinaleño Mountains, all the area above ten thousand feet—roughly eighteen hundred acres—has been set aside as a squirrel refugium, and a team of biologists is on hand from May to November to monitor the squirrels.

*Their* sign is plentiful, too. Lengths of bright pink flagging tape trail off into the forest at intervals, always leading to a midden tree. More flagging and numbered stakes mark each midden site. Other biologists, not connected with the squirrel survey, have set up small wire cages just off the main path. "Seed traps," Steve explains. Before the first winter snowfall, the traps will be emptied. Their contents will give an idea of how many seeds of what kind reach the forest floor, and how this varies from year to year.

Continuing up the trail, we enter another meadow where everything is either huge or tiny. Cow parsnip, with leaves the size of umbrellas and flower heads as big as dinner plates, makes me feel as graceful as a ballerina, yet the delicate flowers of spur gentian, like miniature yellow pagodas, remind me that I am not. Alternately diminutive and gigantic, I am Alice in Wonderland, entirely the wrong size for the landscape I inhabit.

And so the trail goes, in and out of meadow and forest, a line like a story, a rhythm, a tune. John Gardner said that a novelist's primary duty is to maintain the illusion that the fiction he or she tells is real.

When we read a really good novel, Gardner says, "We slip into a dream forgetting it's lunchtime or time to go to work." This is what it should be like to walk in wilderness: to dream that you are the first on the scene, even while knowing that you are not. And, just as an author, by careless language, can jerk the reader from this dream, spoiling all pleasure in it, so the wilderness dream can be spoiled by stray candy wrappers, rusty tin cans, and pieces of foil—any ugly reminder of previous travelers.

Drenched in sunlight from the head down, in dew from the feet up, I am in a kind of dream until the trail dumps us onto a brand new road, so new that straw still litters the right-of-way and survey-ors' stakes remain in the crumbly berm. The road has severed the trail in half. Not only in half, it turns out as we continue on, but in thirds, quarters, eighths, sixteenths. Talk about being jerked from the dream. This is rough footsteps in the night, a banging door, the sound of gunfire. At first bereft, then infuriated, I pull out a stake and fling it into the road. "Watch me turn into Ed Abbey before your very eyes," I tell Steve. He shrugs, not unkindly. Edward Abbey pulled surveyors' stakes to protest the paving of little-traveled roads in na-tional parks. This situation is quite different. An astronomical ob-servatory, now under construction on Emerald Peak, lies less than a mile away. The road goes right to it. What did I expect? He reminds me that we are here on sufferance, by right of a special permit.

It is not long until we reach the construction site, which looks and sounds much like any other site of this kind. A chain link fence, no-trespassing signs, front-end loaders, gravel piles, a house trailer, a water tank, generators, scaffolds, trucks, cranes, welders, and hoses. Men in hard hats shout over the burr of motors and the hiss of com-pressed air.

Once it is completed, the observatory on Mount Graham will be operated by the University of Arizona. Right now it is not much more than a circular cement collar with a lattice of steel on top. Aout eigh-teen hundred spruce trees were cut down to make room for the observatory. Another thirty-two hundred spruce were removed for the new road. The old road to the top of the mountain was not suitable, and the cost of upgrading it was considered too great.

Steve and I cross the construction yard feeling conspicuous: we're the only people wearing packs, the only ones without yellow hard hats. No one challenges us, and we hurry up the trail, pursued by the roar of construction. For a long time it sounds as though we must be near an airport.


We follow a line of flagging tape to a squirrel monitoring station where we find Paul, the biologist in charge, and two of his assistants. He explains that one of their goals is to mark each squirrel with an ear tag. If they can distinguish individual squirrels, they can learn what the sex ratio of the population is, how many females are lactating, how much territory each squirrel explores for food, and even how long the squirrels live.

First they must trap the squirrels, though, and this is proving more difficult than expected. Earlier in the year, before wild mushrooms were plentiful, they tried store-bought mushrooms as bait. No success. Now they are using peanut butter, the old standby, which works as well as anything. Team members observe the traps all day long, so someone is always on hand to tag and release a squirrel as soon as it is caught.

Paul rummages around in a midden, a hummock of cone scales at the base of a dead fir tree. The middens here are not well developed, he tells us. Because the spruce trees produce a good cone crop only once every four years, the middens start to decay before they reach a substantial size. He pulls a few dried, black mushrooms out of the midden. The squirrels collect mushrooms throughout the fall and hang them in the trees to dry, then cache them in middens or in snags. Boletes and amanitas are the kind of mushrooms that seem to be their favorites. In good years, spruce seeds are the staple of their diet, and a squirrel might stash as many as a thousand spruce cones in its pantry. Red squirrels remain active all winter, even with ten or twelve feet of snow on the ground. Without their food caches they would starve.

When the observatory was in the planning stages, conservationists expected that the presence of endangered red squirrels would be enough to stop construction of the observatory; but university administrators, well-versed in the politics of pressure, somehow short-circuited the environmental assessment process. Those of us who cared watched in dismay as Forest Service officials proved oddly passive in shepherding the land and animals under their jurisdiction. We hoped that the U.S. Fish and Wildlife Service, charged with protection of endangered species, could bring the entire project to a halt. The Fish and Wildlife biologists did what they could. Fish and Wildlife required Coronado National Forest to close the Bible camp near Mount Graham; to evict the residents of Columbine, a nearby hamlet of summer homes; to deny public access to the area above ten thousand feet; to rip all roads—except the new one—within the squirrel refugium. These demands ostensibly meant to protect the red squirrels, were regarded by the conservation community as "poison pills," that is, as restrictions so abhorrent to Forest Service officials that the observatory would never be built. Surely the Forest Service would refuse to swallow them. We were wrong. If I was surprised when Forest Service officials agreed to close the Bible camp and the summer homes, I was astonished when they ripped up the roads, for the Forest Service loves roads much more than it loves forests.

The trail ascends by easy stages to Bear Wallow Cienega, a small bog amid the spruce and fir. Sedges and wild onions make a fragrant turf. Moisture seeps everywhere. No matter where we step, the ground sinks underfoot. This is a nivation hollow, a bowl-shaped depression where snow lasts well into May or June. During the summer, the entire hollow becomes a gigantic spring, as if it were a saturated sponge being slowly but steadily expressed. The runoff gradually collects in a single channel, becoming the headwaters of Frye Creek.

Altogether, there are three high–elevation bogs in the Pinaleño Mountains: this one on the flanks of Hawk Peak and two others nearby. These cienegas, unique in southeastern Arizona, are partly a result of topography, partly of the severe winters. Annual precipitation here is about thirty–five inches, 60 percent of it snow.

Paul points out spruce stumps at the edge of the cienega. Some years back, he explains, the Forest Service was concerned lest invading spruce trees turn the cienega to forest, so they cut down many of the big trees at the perimeter. The stumps are broad and flat. I choose a sunny one and sit on it with my knees drawn up while Steve botanizes. Rare wildflowers grow here—white–flowered shooting stars, lady's tresses orchids, marsh marigolds, fringed gentians—and he is as rapt as a fritillary on a thistle.

Like the red squirrels, the marsh marigolds and shooting stars are relics from a colder, moister time when the arid plains below were as verdant and wet as this cienega is now. Tens of thousands of years ago, spruce forests wrapped the entire mountain, not just its highest peaks, and a red squirrel could have scampered the hundred miles between the Pinaleño and the White Mountains without ever coming down from the trees.


After lunch, Paul returns to his monitoring station. Steve and I hike the short distance from Bear Wallow Cienega to the top of Mount Graham, the highest point in southeastern Arizona. As we eat lunch on a smooth log, a small hawk circles around us, showing a checkered tail, then settles at the top of a spruce. It lands elegantly, feet first. As the branch bends underneath its weight, it wavers for a second, then catches its balance. With one fluid motion, it draws its wings down and tucks them in. "Cooper's or sharp–shinned?" I ask. Hoping to draw it closer, I make loud clucks that are meant to be squirrel–like. The hawk ignores me.

"Make a noise like prey," I tell Steve.

He squeals, "Don't eat me, don't eat me, don't eat me."

Mount Graham is not so much a peak as a high spot on a long ridge. Here, where the soil is thin and the winter winds fierce, the spruce forest is dwarfed. Only a few plant species thrive under these stringent conditions. Steve, listing everything he sees, finds no more than a dozen. None is rare, much less endangered.

"I can find no botanical reason *not* to put a telescope here," he says.

That may be, I argue, but the best reason not to erect telescopes on this high peak is spiritual, not scientific.

"I have no expertise in that area," he says.

But of course he does. He is embarrassed to talk about it, that's all. Good at assembling objective evidence, scientists are sometimes apt to shrink from matters of the heart. At his heart right now is the plight of this silent forest—the moss, the trees, the stony outcrops, the winds. He wonders aloud if every high peak must bear some human marker: a fire lookout, a gaggle of radio towers, a microwave station, a ski lift, an observatory. Are we to have no mountaintops left unbroken?

I tell him about Robert Leonard Reid, who acted on his boyhood love of stars by submitting an application to Harvard's prestigious astronomy program. He was thrilled to be accepted. "I'd dreamed of intimacy with Andromeda," he writes, "but had always imagined she was unattainable. Now suddenly I had been handed the keys to her apartment!"

The reality was somewhat different. For the next six months he sat at the controls of the telescope, photographing the sky instead of gazing at it. By the time he saw the stars, he writes, "they were white splotches on a sheet of emulsion." The splotches, he was told, represented rotating nuclear reactions converting hydrogen to helium. When he finally left the program, he was sadly disillusioned. He concluded that science had discarded not only sight, sound, taste, touch, and smell, but soul as well.

We return to our truck via the ripped road. It is strange to see a road so humped and hollowed and distorted. Steve speculates that a bulldozer dug it up with enormous steel prongs. Walking the road requires a peculiar kind of stutter step, and I feel like I'm wearing a high-heeled shoe on one foot and no shoe at all on the other.

Wild raspberries grow thick beside the roadway. We sample the ripening fruits: every tenth one is sweet and good, the rest insipid or tart. The juncos like them, though, and as we approach, they flee by the dozen from every bush with alarmed rustling of wings. Listening to them, I realize that I do not agree with Robert Leonard Reid. Science is my eyes, my fingers, and my ears. It is my window on the world, a window I will take with me no matter where we move.

# 12 from botanist to bagworm lady

The Chiricahua Mountains are a big, capacious range. Their canyons are deep, their forests are wide. Rucker Canyon, carved from
the southern flank of the range, emphatically belongs to this over-
sized place—long enough and wide enough to occupy even the ca-
sual visitor for a day.

I am here with a group from the Arizona Native Plant Society, and
we are seated on a streamside bank under willows and pines, eating
our sack lunches. It is a weekend workshop, that staple of nonprofit
nature societies everywhere, and I am supposed to be a botanical
trip leader. At the moment, having just spied a bagworm hanging
from a willow branch overhead, I am about to abandon botany for
entomology.

Although I have never seen a bagworm before, I know it instantly
from illustrations in books. "'Tis a consummation devoutly to be
wished," as Hamlet said; I have always wanted to see a bagworm
in the wild. This particular bagworm is three or four feet above my

head and looks like a clump of dead leaves. By pulling down the supple branch hand over hand, I bring the bagworm within reach, then break off its twig and let the branch fly back up.

Bagworms are moth caterpillars that spin cocoons for protection. My bagworm's cocoon is four inches long and about as thick as a child's fist. The silken tube is concealed by a dense spiral of dried, brown willow leaves and fine twigs. I tuck it into my lunch sack, removing the orange first so that the cocoon won't be crushed or damaged.

Later in the day, I show it to an entomologist, another trip leader, who confirms that it is a bagworm. He says, "That's a good find." Bagworms belong to the family Psychidae, he tells me. There are about twenty species of bagworms in the United States and Canada. He adds that the bag is empty; the caterpillar has already metamorphosed into a moth. That is fine with me; for one reason or another I have raised more than my share of caterpillars, and I do not relish the idea of trying to find willow leaves for this one once I return home to the desert. I put the sack in a corner of my cabin and think no more about it.

That night, I am on the verge of sleep when a rustling noise startles me wide awake. Oh no. Mice. Peg Bracken says that when someone starts a sentence with the words, "It's a funny thing about me," you will in all likelihood be able to control your mirth. "They are only getting ready to announce the shattering fact that they don't like something," she says. "And it's not going to be something that's really quite awful, like suttee or apartheid; it's going to be something small." You will not be startled, therefore, when I tell you that it's a funny thing about me, but I cannot sleep when I hear mice.

Camping in Utah a few summers ago, for instance, I was nearly asleep when I heard the whisper of tiny feet on plastic. This was a canoe trip, so all my food was in dry bags, flexible waterproof sacks manufactured especially for canoeists, kayakers, and rafters. Dry bags are expensive enough that I did not want mice chewing holes through mine.

I unzipped my sleeping bag, unzipped the tent, crawled out with my flashlight between my teeth, suspended all the bags from a nearby oak tree, and went back to bed. I had just drifted to sleep when the rustling began again. I sighed. My sleeping bag was warm, the night was chilly, and perhaps the mice would go away of their own accord. They did not. Eventually, I crawled out of the tent again and examined the dry bags. They seemed fine—no punctures, no scratches, no rodent droppings. Still, the rustling continued all night long, and I did not sleep a wink.

It was a bleary-eyed dawn. Heating water for coffee, I stared dully into the middle distance, which happened to include my plastic garbage bag, also suspended from the oak tree. The bag rustled, then jumped, then rustled again. Cautiously, I lowered the bag, opened it wide. The fattest mouse I had ever seen in my life waddled out. It had spent the night devouring the better part of a loaf of moldy bread.

All this runs through my head as I lie listening from my bed in the cabin. The blankets are warm, the floor is cold, but I know I will get no sleep until I find the mouse and cease its infernal rustling. It's a funny thing about me. I throw back the blankets and turn on the light. First, I examine the sack of groceries, opening each cracker and cereal box in turn. No mouse. I poke through the carton of books and file folders. No mouse there either. I empty out my backpack, then shake out my boots. Still no mouse. I go back to bed. The rustling resumes. Clearly, I am doomed to another sleepless night.

Next evening, back at home, I am reading quietly when I hear a scratching noise. It is the same sound that kept me awake in the cabin. Skin prickling just a bit, I put my book down. Have I somehow managed to bring a mouse home? Are mice to be a recurring motif all my life? Then an awful surmise strikes me. I open my lunch sack. There is the bagworm, inching around inside like some kind of Gothic horror, not departed at all but very much alive.

Although it will be a nuisance to keep it supplied with willow leaves, I am not displeased to have the chance to raise another caterpillar. Not displeased, that is, until I look up *Bagworm* in my field guide to insects. With dismay I learn of its peculiar habits. The caterpillar feeds while protected by its cocoon. It pupates inside the bag too. The pupa is the resting stage in the life of a moth or butterfly. After a few weeks, the male moth emerges from the cocoon and spends its brief life searching for female moths. The female is legless and wingless. She stays inside her cocoon, and that is where the male finds her and mates with her. According to my book, "she then lays eggs inside the bag, exits, and dies."

Great, just great. Either I can hatch out a male that will spend its few days in a futile search for females, or I can hatch out a female that will wait hopelessly for a mate at the bottom of her bag. The whole thing smacks of Sylvia Plath. Let's all stick our heads in the oven and turn on the gas now.

I call my entomologist friend, leave a long and complicated message with his wife, but he never calls back. No doubt he has some idea of what lies ahead.


Meantime, I stick the willow twig into a big pickle jar and balance the bagworm cocoon on the twig. I place a piece of wire screen on top of the jar and put the whole arrangement on a narrow shelf beside the dining room table. The next morning, the bagworm has positioned itself in a hanging position, which is fine, but the willow leaves are dried out. The closest source of willows I can recall at this moment is a thirty-minute drive followed by a forty-minute walk. I call my office and tell them I will be late. The morning is hot, and there are hungry mosquitoes by the creek. A traffic jam on the way home adds another ten minutes to my travel time. But having removed the poor creature from its natural habitat, it seems the least I can do.

In the evening, the bagworm seems discontented. It lurches around inside the jar, dragging its bag behind it like a dirty diaper, unwilling or unable to feed upon the fresh leaves. The caterpillar itself is about as thick as a pencil and dark brown. I catch a glimpse of its head and upper body once or twice as it crawls about. As soon as it sees me, it ducks inside its bag with a guilty, furtive movement, like a child snatching her hand from a cookie jar.

The next day, I come home for lunch. The pickle jar is empty. The piece of wire screen lies on the table. The bagworm is nowhere in sight. I look on the shelf, the table, the chairs. No bagworm. And then I see it in the middle of the floor. It has crawled halfway across the room. Fortunately, I had not stepped on it when I came in.

I put the bagworm back into the jar, replace the wire screen, and put a heavy stapler on top. That should hold it, I decide, and go back to the office. When I return home in the evening, the jar is empty, and the screen and stapler are both on the table. Clearly, this is no ordinary insect. Harry Houdini has come back from the dead, and he is a bagworm. I search for some time before I find it crawling up the window frame. I watch as the caterpillar elongates its upper body, then hitches up its cocoon with a great effort. It is like watching someone climb a cliff while wearing a sleeping bag.

Despairing of its happiness and mine, I take the bagworm outdoors and place it in the crook of the mulberry tree. Silk worms eat mulberry leaves, I reason, so perhaps a bagworm will too. Later, I notice that it has made its way halfway down the trunk. It is clinging to the rough bark and peering anxiously over its shoulder as if to sight out the easiest route down. By evening it has reached the base of the tree and, no doubt exhausted, has suspended itself in a resting position among the flower pots.


The next evening the bagworm is not where I had last seen it. At length I discover it on one of the main branches. Over the course of the day it has migrated five feet vertically and four feet horizontally. It isn't going anywhere when I find it, however. A twig, pressing against the cocoon, keeps the worm from moving despite its valiant efforts. I remember a turtle my daughter once had. This turtle used to crawl headfirst into a corner, then flail its little limbs while making no forward progress whatsoever. The turtle died at an early age. I resolve to return my bagworm to the mountains in the morning.

I don't sleep well. It's a funny thing about me, but I cannot sleep when I know there is a bagworm starving in my backyard. I am outside at first light. Naturally, the bagworm is not where I last saw it. I search casually at first, then systematically, dividing the canopy into quarters and staring upwards at each one in turn. I look on the ground among the fallen leaves and sticks and flower pots. I have no love of ladders or heights, but I climb to the roof of the house and look down on the tree from above. The bagworm is nowhere to be found. Perhaps it has crawled through the chain link fence into the neighbor's yard. Perhaps it has been destroyed by birds. Perhaps it has achieved some final apotheosis in which bag and worm ascended to heaven in a chariot of fire. After half an hour I give up and go for my morning walk, but the angular feeling of a good deed left undone sticks in my throat.

I make a final search before I leave for the office, and there it is, suspended from a leafy twig high overhead. By standing on a step-ladder, I am able to snip off the twig with a long-handled pruning shears, and it tumbles into my arms. The cocoon is tightly fastened by a loop of silk that winds around and around the branch. The mouth of the bag has collapsed shut. This, I predict confidently to myself, is a caterpillar that has put itself to bed once and for all. It is pupating inside the bag, and when it emerges again, it will be a moth. What better time to return it to the wild? I place the mulberry twig and the pendant cocoon inside a shoe box, then call the office to let them know I will be late again.

It is a lovely morning for a drive to the mountains. I know exactly where I am headed: a deep canyon in the Santa Catalina Mountains with pine trees and wild grapes on the slopes and a profusion of willows along the creek. It will take me about forty-five minutes to get there. Windows down, radio up, I head for the Catalina Highway.

Before long, I hear a rustling noise from inside the box but resolve to ignore it. It's just the cocoon swinging from the branch, I tell myself. Not to worry. You will not look up to find a bagworm inching across the windshield, signaling passing cars for rescue.

Having reached my destination, I park the car beside the creek. Gratefully, I see that the willows are as thick as I remembered. I peer inside the box. The bagworm peers back. We eye one another a final time before it pops inside its bag and clutches the opening shut. I search for a good willow, one with plenty of tender new leaves, then put the cocoon in place.

Juncos chatter from the pines nearby. A chipmunk perches on a fallen log, then darts away. As I turn to leave, I glance into the branches of a chokecherry and see a clump of dead willow leaves. It is a bagworm cocoon, of course. Somehow I have managed to reach the age of forty-two without ever having seen a bagworm, and now they are all over the place.

I pluck it from the branch. The silken tube is gray and weathered and split. There is definitely nothing inside. I put it in the shoe box. Now this is what I call a good find.

# high summer in heaven *13*

The cabins at Columbine are painted either green or brown, muddy Forest Service colors meant to blend with the landscape, I suppose. All have tin roofs, and a few have smoking chimneys, a cozy sight on this chilly August morning. Two little girls in dresses play outside one cabin. As Steve and I pass, the younger says in a singsong voice, "This is our cabin. This is our cabin."

The other calls, "Daddy, Daddy," and a clean-cut man in his early thirties, wearing well-worn jeans and a denim jacket, comes around from the back of the house. He politely directs us to the Ash Creek Trail, which we have somehow missed.

Earlier I wondered if I would recognize the cabin where, years ago, my first husband and I, along with our friends John and Cathy, sheltered during an October storm. No one was living there then, and the place was boarded up. We huddled on the front porch until the rain stopped. Now, as Steve and I pass the last cabin on the road, I do recognize it, more by position than by appearance.

Ash Creek rises near here—its source, in the common parlance. Except that, as Steve points out, *source* is a misnomer, since a river or stream has many sources—all the tributaries that feed into it along its journey. Ash Creek is one of six perennial streams in the Pinaleño Mountains, which are unusually well watered for southeastern Arizona. In the Santa Catalina Mountains, only Lemmon Creek is perennial, and then only in certain reaches. The Rincon Mountains have no perennial streams, nor do the Sierritas, the Baboquivaris, the Whetstones, the Tucsons, or the Tortolitas. In a dry season, you can walk a long way for a little water.

Extraordinarily clear, extraordinarily cold, Ash Creek in its upper reaches drops steeply over rounded, moss-backed boulders. The drops are brief, the pools so tiny that a child could leap them. A kind of toy stream. In Yorkshire it would be called a *beck*. American English does not bother to make the distinction. A hydrologist might call it a *stepped-bed stream* or refer to its *chute-and-pool topography*.

As a child, I would have loved this place, plopping myself down beside the creek and entering immediately an imaginary world of enchanted fish, bejeweled trees, and talking waters. Now that I am an adult, I remember this world only in snatches, as when, unprepared for a sudden, cold rain in the mountains, Steve and I sought shelter in a leafy cave of silverleaf oaks. After fire, these forest trees resprout as many-stemmed clumps, and this is where we found a hiding place: in an opening somehow carved out amid a clump. We entered on hands and knees. There was just enough room inside for the two of us to sit with heads bent and legs bunched up. Outside, rain pounded on the canopy. Inside, we were dry, if shivery. We huddled together on the fallen leaves like Hansel and Gretel, a little worried yet perfectly safe.

Clumps of a cornlike plant lean over the stream. The stalks are as tall as I am, the leaves as large as my face. Ordinarily, the leaves are stiffly cupped. You could use them as soup bowls if they weren't poisonous. Here the leaves show damage from a recent storm. Many are uncupped, and tattered as if pelted by hailstones.

"*Veratrum californicum*," Steve says thoughtfully. "What is its common name, do you know?" He has a million Latin names at his disposal, which leaves little room in his brain for the English ones.

I suggest skunk cabbage, which he does not like. Skunk cabbage to him will always be *Lysichitum americanum*, a bog plant of second-growth forests in the Pacific Northwest.

"False hellebore," he says, suddenly remembering another possibility, but I do not care for its philosophical implications. We agree finally on corn lily, a suitable name because the inflorescence looks like outsize corn tassels.

When we stop talking, the only sound is the clatter of water falling from pool to pool. The boulders are steely gray where wet, dark brown where dry. They give the stream its stair–step topography: water pools atop one boulder, then cascades down its face and pools atop the next. Kneeling by the water, I remember other streams with other sounds: the trainlike rumble of a desert wash in full flood, the barely audible rustle of a creek meandering through sedge and grass. The topography and the music are not unrelated of course. Most desert washes run infrequently, but when they do run, the volume of water is apt to be great enough that rocks the size of basketballs tumble and bang together. At first this cold water seems quite sterile, but after a minute I see tiny, scrambling beetles and caddisfly larvae in cases fashioned from spruce needles and bits of bark. They pay me no mind as my face looms over them; I could be looking through one–way glass.

For the first few miles, the trail is an old dirt road now closed to vehicles. The forest towers to either side—tall, gray trunks of Engelmann spruce and white fir mostly, with a few white pine. Pale sunlight slants between the trunks and across the forest floor, making a barred landscape: bars of tree, bars of shadow, bars of light.

Along the bank of the road, spruce and fir saplings jockey for position. They grow quickly along the road, where light is plentiful, more slowly back in the forest, where the sun does not so easily reach. When we step off the road, we can walk unhindered between trees, while overhead the branches of adjacent spruces and firs meet and mingle, weaving a thick screen between the sky and the forest floor.

This predominance of spruce and fir has ramifications for every other organism that shares their space. Low light makes the understory sparse: no shrubs, no grasses, only a few shade–loving orchids. Lack of understory means that most animal activity is restricted either to the thick litter, where shrews hunt for grubs, or to the upper layers of the forest, where chickadees glean for insects and red squirrels forage for spruce cones.

Columbines harvest their share of light by growing along the stream. Their blossoms are pale yellow, their spurs extravagantly long. Nectar tubes is what the spurs are, and if you pinch off the tip of one between your teeth, you might receive the tiniest bit of sweetness on your tongue. Minuscule flies cluster on the anthers, eating pollen perhaps. I chase them away and inhale the sweet and lemony fragrance of the blossoms. The touch of lemon is not unexpected in a moth–pollinated flower. Only moths with long tongues—sphinx or hawk moths—can reach the nectar in the tips of these spurs.

As we amble down the trail, I try to remember from sixteen years ago what is coming up next. The road, I recall, leads to the site of a sawmill, and about that point the stream is stocked with trout. John and Phil tried their luck with salmon eggs and earthworms. I don't think anyone caught anything. That was a chilly, misty October day. Low clouds drifted up the canyon, weaving in and out of yellow aspens, blurring the canyon slopes, wrapping a persistent chill around our necks and shoulders.

A tree has fallen across the road. It is too big to clamber over conveniently, so we skirt it at the downhill end, noticing that when it toppled, it took some substrate with it. Now that the roots are exposed, we can see how they grew around rocks, accommodating and imprisoning them. Some of these fallen giants are still as hard and solid as the day they fell. Others, especially those in contact with the earth, are rotten. Tiny spruces, none more than six inches high, have sprouted in the crumbling, cinnamon–colored wood. In this moist and humid environment, a tree has ramifications even after it dies. Its decay releases nutrients and organic matter, a boon to a community in which a high proportion of both is bound up in the wood and needles of living trees. Until it rots completely, a fallen tree may be a safe haven for seeds and seedlings of Engelmann spruce. The seeds, wedged into cracks, are more likely to escape the sharp noses of rodents, and the seedlings are less apt to be drifted over by leaf litter or trampled underfoot. Fallen logs represent a spruce seedling's best chance to become a permanent member of the forest.

When we reach the mill site, a meadowy clearing in the forest, it is not quite as I remembered it—not as broad, not as flat, not as scarred by roads. No buildings remain, but we find many old pieces of rusted equipment half-hidden by grasses and wildflowers: a boiler; a length of pipe, badly corroded; a section of gear far too heavy for me to lift even though it represents no more than a quarter of the original wheel; and other metal objects whose original use is not at all obvious. So obscure is their intention, in fact, that I find it easier to think of them in terms of sculpture—as objects possessing a certain heft and shape and color—than as components of a manufactory.

High summer in the mountains. The meadow is sunny and green and flecked with butterflies and flowers. Steve makes a plant list: sneezeweed, orchard grass, elderberry, skyrocket, and dozens more. Down by the creek, red monkey flowers clamber up the bank. Tiger swallowtails glide over the stream, tip-tilting like small yellow kites, and the inevitable painted ladies bask on damp sand. Is this summer, or is it heaven? I had been prepared to condemn the greed that could erect a sawmill in this place, but now—awash in butterflies and wildflowers—I cannot work up much righteous indignation.

The child I was would have loved this, too, and in a different way than I do now. Children have a particular relationship with landscape that adults somehow lose. John Jerome writes that the last place he knew with a child's intimacy was a small farm in New Braunfels, Texas. "I was sixteen when we moved there," he says, "and knew at the time that I was already a couple of years too old to 'play' on it in the way that would have revealed its true intimacy to me."

The last place I knew that well was the orange grove and vacant lot behind my parents' house, *vacant* being a term that only an adult would have applied to that intricate and lively world. Bindweed clambered across the furrows, sunflowers grew as tall as small trees, and wild radish bloomed in pink and white profusion. At one end of the lot, two peach trees grew in an apron of garlic. I would climb to the lowest fork of one and sit there for hours, singing at the top of my voice and inhaling the scent of freshly bruised garlic. By the age of twenty, all this was lost to me. On visits back home, I would wander across the lot and wonder why it seemed so remote. So vacant.

Peering into the stream, Steve sees several small trout: "There aren't many, and they're not big," he says. A slight motion of my hand drives them all for cover. The stream bed, less steep here than it was above, has assumed the pool–and–riffle topography so beloved of trout fishermen. Alternating silence and song, water lazes in the pools, which are deep and nearly level, speeds through the cobbled stretches, which are shallow and tilted. "These might be *Salmo apache*, the native Apache trout," Steve says. When he adds that it is a threatened species, I remember the fishing trip of sixteen years ago and cringe. Few of us thought in terms of threatened or endangered species then.

Alder and aspen border the stream. The alders are graceful trees with smooth, pale gray bark and neatly scalloped leaves. Awkwardly branched, somewhat contorted, the aspens are less graceful but no less beautiful, especially now when every branchlet twinkles with its pendant green leaf. Both aspen and alder are relatively short-lived trees. Their strategy is to grow fast, die young, and leave a lot of offspring to colonize clearings in the conifer forest. The logging of spruce and fir many years ago gave them an ideal opening here.

And not only them. A black-and-white butterfly—a Wiedemeyer's admiral—circles around and around through the topmost branches of the alders. Rising above the treetops, the butterfly skims through a cloud of gnats. Possibly it is a male searching for a mate, showing his colors as an advertisement for himself. Like most butterflies, the Wiedemeyer's admiral loves sunny clearings; it would seldom if ever penetrate the dense conifer forest upstream.

Steve remarks, "If there were plans to put a sawmill here now, we'd be up in arms." As it is, he continues, past disturbance has created variability in the habitat, and it is the variability to which we respond. An ecologist would call it "patchiness," this mosaic of meadow, stream, and forest. It startles us to realize that many decades later, the logging of upper Ash Canyon has produced these unexpected benefits. Impossible, really, to weigh the damp conifer forest against this airy meadow; impossible to say whether one is better, the other worse. It's enough to make me hopeful—almost—about moving. Surely a similar process would occur in my life, and with time (and with explorations on foot and in books), the new place would prove as rich as the old.

I make a list of butterflies to complement Steve's list of plants; it is our way of getting a handle on the variability we treasure. Evidently neither of us can enjoy the beauties of nature without cataloging and categorizing them. My friend Barbara, a novelist, told me that someone accused her of turning everything into a story. Biologists do the same, only we turn everything into science. Did logging remove the trees that would be today's fallen logs? If so, does that mean logging has affected the nutrient cycle of the forest? What about establishment of conifer seedlings? Are there now fewer seedlings than you might find in a comparable unlogged forest? Someone overhearing our talk might wonder why we cannot enjoy the beauties of nature in silence. But for us, nature is these connections, and her beauty lies in the way they fit together. In the days when I knew John and Cathy, I was too old to play on the vacant lot, too young to have found any other point of entry. Now I have done so: talking with the natural world, I have managed to recapture that earlier intimacy.

Steve and I stop in the meadow to catch our breath. Now, in late afternoon, the sun has sunk behind the ridge, and the air is cooling rapidly. All the butterflies have decamped, seeking shelter wherever it is that butterflies spend the night. Under leaves, I expect. Maybe at night you could creep under an alder tree, snap on your flashlight and see a quivering canopy of upside-down butterflies overhead.

I remember now, that while the men fished, Cathy and I rambled downstream through mist and golden aspen. I remember the blue-green forest of the slopes, the deep quiet that absorbed our voices and footsteps. We came to a waterfall, or at least a water slide. Slick Rock Falls, it is called—a vast, slanting sheet of bedrock one hundred feet high. Then, the stream slipped down the center of the sheet as docilely as if released from the end of a garden hose. During snowmelt, though, it must shoot off the lip, surging into the air and tumbling as if from buckets to the stream bed below.

When it started to sprinkle, Cathy and I headed back up the trail, huffing and puffing. Was it here or somewhere else that Cathy told me the secret to hiking steep grades? "Let the men race ahead if they want," she said. "This is the way I go up big hills." And she showed me: methodical baby steps, slow but easy on heart and lungs and quadriceps. That's how I've climbed hills ever since, with no apologies to anyone.

By the time we caught up with our husbands, the shower had turned to rain, and by the time the four of us returned to the trail head, we were all soaked. The road was too wet and slick for our car, so we took refuge on the porch of the nearest cabin. Cold and shivering, all conversation spent, we waited in silence. When the rain finally stopped, we left. The car had barely enough gasoline for the trip back down the mountain, and we coasted much of the way in neutral.

Pulling into a service station with a teaspoonful of gas in the tank, we felt lucky and cocky as if we would be young and strong forever.

I know better now, but it took me more than twenty years to learn it. Twenty years and hundreds of miles on trails. As students of comparative religion already know, almost any comparison tells you more than you knew before, whether you compare chimpanzee with human bones, fossil with modern plant distributions, or desert scrub in Arizona with desert scrub in Argentina. Now, comparing the person I was when I first made this hike with the person I am now, I see the effect of place. Then, I was undisciplined, impulsive, and unfocused, showing little promise of living up to whatever potential I might have had. In these mountains, and because of them, I have developed a scientist's outlook and a botanist's skills. I have learned discipline and have acquired about as much patience as I can tolerate. No one could have anticipated these changes; they were the mysterious result of place knocking against personality, shaping it and smoothing some of the rougher angles. Realizing this, I almost look forward to watching myself react to and interact with a new place, should we move, and twenty years afterward to assessing the ways in which it changed me.

# looking into clear water 14

Late last summer, Steve and I waded through chest-high wildflowers and butterflies to get past the mouth of this little side canyon. It is a tributary to Box Canyon, which is itself not so much a canyon as a pass. Parting the stems with our hands, reluctant to tread so much beauty underfoot, we made slow progress down the stream bed as thousands of butterflies—skippers, painted ladies, red-rimmed satyrs, queens, and Mexican snouts—rose in waves, then closed ranks behind us.

No such luck on this September afternoon. Butterflies are few, and the wildflowers, *Bidens aurea*—slender, yellow sunflowers that thrive on late summer moisture—evidently do not intend to bloom. It looks as if summer rains skipped this part of the Santa Rita Mountains. That happens sometimes; a battalion of storms batters the desert week after week, and only your garden, it seems, is missed. Over five years or a decade, it all evens out.

Steve announces his intention of botanizing on the hillslope. Without much enthusiasm, I continue upstream, just killing time until he is ready to leave.

My thoughts drift away, as they often do these days, to the prospect of moving. Today, I feel a glimmer of excitement at the idea of exploring unknown country: new plants and new animals, or, at the very least, new arrangements of familiar plants and animals. Sometimes, despite what John Jerome so wisely says, you can't renew the old simply by seeing it in a new way. Sometimes you just have to get up and go where you can see something new. This observation has particular force in this particular season and this particular place, where heat and drought have apparently dried up most signs of life.

More gully than gorge, the side canyon winds between gentle hills dotted with oak and juniper. Like a line of coarse basting stitches, a rivulet of water appears and disappears in the wash. An intermittent stream in time as well as in space: in another month or two, it will be gone. In fact, I wonder that it has lasted this long. The water is tepid, a pleasant contrast to the icy stream in Ash Creek. No place is the rivulet so wide that I must stretch my legs to step across. I follow the trickle, expecting it to disappear altogether in another minute or two.

Instead, I come to a basin-sized pool where whirligig beetles dance like droplets on a hot griddle. Because their eyes lie right at the water's surface, they can see above and below the water at the same time, which is perhaps why they notice me well before I see them. They respond as if to a potential predator, with the erratic tarantella that makes them so hard to capture. You'd think they would crash into one another, but they never do, any more than fish in a school or gnats in a swarm. This is because a whirligig beetle swims *within* the water's surface tension, surrounding itself with concentric circles that nudge the circles of nearby beetles, like bumper cars in an electrified arena.

As I watch, one beetle separates itself from the others and describes dreamy loops on the water, ending each with a sharp little pirouette. Its shiny, black body, widest at the middle and tapering to a point at either end, casts a black shadow on the bottom of the pool, an undulating oval that augments and diminishes as it travels over hills and hollows in the sand.

"I'll catch up," I call to Steve, who is poking among the rocks on the hillside. "I'm just going to stop here and make a few notes." He nods, well aware that "a few notes" could mean anything from several lines to half a dozen pages. Maybe he will see me again today, maybe he won't.

I pull my notebook out of my pack. Henry James said a novelist should be one on whom nothing is lost. A naturalist, too, I presume. A difficult goal, since the human mind can manage at most seven simultaneous bits of information, or so I've read: a tone, a word, a color, a touch. Anything over this rather modest limit goes unseen, unheard, unfelt, unthought. Thus the value of notebooks.

A water strider shoots away from me, executes a gliding turn, then stops. The dimples where its feet touch the water make four fat shadows on the bottom of the pool. It seems that water striders propel themselves without expending energy, but if you look closely, you can see them stroke their middle pair of legs like oars, while the front and back pairs remain rigid. Like a white-water rafter, they row from front to back. The rigid legs provide stability, like outriggers. They turn by stroking with one of the middle legs while using a rear leg on the opposite side as a rudder.

As bits of flotsam drift into the pool, the water strider darts after them. Anything too small to represent an immediate threat counts as a potential meal and must be investigated. I seldom see them catch anything and often wonder how they survive. Perhaps their metabolism is so slow that a very occasional meal suffices.

Ambling upstream, I find a garter snake resting on dried grass stems, its yellow and cream stripes a nearly perfect camouflage. In a deep cistern, a bunch of tadpoles cling to the rock wall like kids hanging onto the edge of a swimming pool. A dragonfly nymph scoots across the bottom, then champs its jaws with palpable satisfaction. They move by jet propulsion, pulling water into their body cavities through the anus, then squirting it out forcefully. The same mechanism serves double duty as breathing apparatus: oxygenated water pulled into the body aerates their internal gills.

By living on the bottom, dragonfly and damselfy nymphs avoid the keen competition for food that takes place on the water's surface. Water striders, able to breathe atmospheric oxygen only, are not so fortunate. Some insects, like predacious diving beetles and water boatmen, have the best of both worlds. Because they carry their oxygen supply with them like scuba divers, they can take advantage of food throughout the water column. When they taxi to the surface and pause for a moment or two before sinking again, they are gathering air. It diffuses under their wing covers and into the spaces between innumerable, fine body hairs.

This seems a ludicrously *ad hoc* arrangement, but improvisation is to be expected given that aquatic insects evolved from terrestrial ones. Adapting land-based parts for use in water, they turned feet into paddles and tracheae into gills. Somehow, it all works. With their portable bubbles, some aquatic insects can spend six or eight hours underwater without resurfacing. Even a three-day stint is not impossible given the proper conditions.

Underwater, a garter snake noses among scattered stones like a dog sniffing out quarry. It scares up a tadpole, which shoots across the pool, then freezes in place. Randomly speckled with olive gray and pink, the tadpole has a leathery look, like the cover of a Bible, and blends in beautifully with its randomly speckled background. In another pool, a gordian worm—an animated noodle—twists and turns. Knotting and unknotting, threading itself back and forth through the water, it looks exactly as if a garter snake's stripe had somehow become detached and taken on a life of its own. Like many worms, it is parasitic. I remember the first time I saw gordian worms. Steve called, "You've got to come see this, it's really disgusting," then showed me a fist-sized mass of slender worms all knotted and tangled like boiled spaghetti.

What is it about looking down into clear water that fascinates us so? We peer into water as if it had something to tell us, something other than a narcissistic reflection of our own beauty. When Steve and I paddle our canoe around the margins of a lake, I never tire of gazing into the wavering forests of water plants. Each slender, twining stem, tangled among a dozen others, is clearly visible, as are the small beetles that cling to them, swaying up and down with the motion of our silent passage. It's like watching television, in a way. Both involve the perception of movement behind an interposed surface, which seems to exert a hypnotic attraction of its own.

As I continue upstream, queens—rusty orange butterflies dotted with white—spring from patches of damp sand. A dragonfly with a turquoise thorax and black abdomen lands on a grass blade. Its wings are so clear they are invisible except when they catch the light and glimmer like cellophane. I hold my breath involuntarily, as if the slightest current of air will scare it off. Absolute attention is prayer, said Simone Weil. At this moment I know what she meant. I am magnetized, and the stream pulls me onward. Mottled granite surfaces under my feet, then gradually rises into a staircase of polished rock, a miniature gorge where running water has scoured deep pockets. They brim and overflow; the water is cool and dark.

Who would have thought that a seasonal stream could have so much life in it? I have found a dozen species during a single afternoon; an aquatic biologist, sampling over the course of several summers, might uncover a hundred. Wherever water exists, living creatures will somehow make use of it, whether it is permanent or not. Ephemeral waters give rise to ephemeral life cycles. Some aquatic insects—the mayflies and certain true flies—develop from egg to adult within one to three weeks. They reproduce continuously until the water dries up. Others, somewhat more conservative, take from four to eight weeks for development and reproduce only after spring and summer rains fill temporary streams. Deeper pools, which hold water year-round, are reservoirs where frogs and dragonfly larvae and other long-lived species outlast the rainless months.

I have no idea what time it is nor how long I have been gone. There must be some physiological explanation for this state of mind, something to do with alpha waves and right brains. It is the same state we reach when immersed in some activity we love—drawing, writing, looking at a painting, listening to a symphony, or reading a novel. If I could suspend myself in this state of mind, I would stay here forever. But I can't, and even if I could, Steve would still be waiting for me, so I tuck my notebook into my pack and head back toward the truck.

I think again of Henry James, whose notebooks are filled with conversations, story ideas, and snippets of description. They constitute a novelist's working diary, directed toward the incidents and characters that had significance for his craft. My notebooks, filled with butterflies, wildflowers, water beetles, and garter snakes, show what is significant to me. Perhaps what James meant was not that we must take in everything around us all the time; perhaps he was suggesting that significance lurks in unexpected places.

As I round a bend in the gully, I see our truck parked in the shade of a big juniper. Steve is leaning against the fender, relaxed. When I walk up, he is listening to a baseball game on the radio. He did not find much in bloom on the canyon slopes, he says—too dry. Enumerating my discoveries, I realize that a third person might guess we had spent the afternoon in different states, not within shouting distance in the same small gully. It's a great comfort to have accessory interests. I can always find something to look at out-of-doors. Steve, whose love is for plants and plants alone, is more limited, and a dry summer causes him real pain.

By giving me a pair of binoculars six or seven years ago, he encouraged me to branch out. I sometimes wonder if I would still be turning to nature for entertainment if he had not. We become as habituated to our pleasures as to our vices, it seems, and every so often we must increase the dose if we are to attain the same level of stimulation.

Or increase our attention. The seven-bit limit remains, but we decide which seven bits will occupy our minds at any given moment. We attend to what we value; we value what we attend to. Just as snowmelt trickling down through hundreds of feet of rocks and gravels eventually fills a stream-bed pool, so our attention, spaced across hundreds and thousands of hours and days, eventually fills our lives. Clearly, I need to be as careful with my attention as I am with my food: if I choose Coca-Cola instead of fruit juice, televisions instead of lakes, it will make a difference in my life.

Steve starts the truck. The next time we come back here, if we ever do, it will be different from today, just as today was different from last summer. What remains is its significance, and that is something I can take with me no matter where we move.

# 15

gifts given and received

"Isn't this a lovely oak forest?" Steve asks. He is surprisingly cheerful, considering that he submitted his tenure package a day or two ago. The sheer relief of getting it done has buoyed his spirits, I suppose. Now there is nothing more we can do except wait. In another nine months we will know the verdict.

He's quite right. It is a lovely forest. All the trees are Arizona oaks. Their trunks are short and knotted, and their leaves are gray–green, a somber hue. The woodland floor is a jumble of reddish–brown leaves and angular boulders. Sunlight skips through the branches and dapples the ground. As wind stirs the canopy, black shadows of oak leaves shiver on gray rocks.

The air and earth are damp from rain, and beads of moisture seep from the saw-toothed leaves of wild strawberry. There are so many wildflowers it seems more like August than late September: two kinds of wild geranium, one magenta, the other white; wild flax, as blue as tropical seas; twining morning glories with white throats and pink lips; and wild beans, growing from tubers the size of filberts.

This portion of the Santa Catalina Mountains is a system of parallel canyons and ridges laid out side by side like a bony hand—Oracle Ridge, Samaniego Ridge, Red Ridge, and the Reef of Rock. Our view from Oracle Ridge takes in hundreds of square miles of mountain and desert. In the valley far below, a thick green cord of trees hides the San Pedro River. An umbilical cord, as far as I am concerned, but not for my daughter Heather, who has come hiking with us today as a kind of farewell gift before she moves to Pennsylvania. (Her gift to us.)

Her talk as we hike is mainly of her plans for the coming year. For the first time in her life, she will be on her own, living in Pittsburgh ("a *real* city," she says), supporting herself with a full-time job. She wants to live alone for a change: "No more roommates." Quickly she adds that of course if apartments prove too expensive, she'll have to share. Most of her books will stay behind in storage, along with her futon, her television, her bureau, her full-length mirror. So much to do before she leaves, so little time left.

She feels less ambivalent about leaving than I do. One reason is that her interests don't attach her here as strongly as mine. She is a psychology major, and the locational bias of biology exerts few claims on her. All her friends are dispersing too—the great annual exodus of recent graduates. That's a second reason.

"I'll miss my things, especially the books," she says, "but I can't see shipping them all the way to Pittsburgh when I might be leaving for graduate school in a year or two."

Our progress is dilatory. We stop to look at everything. Goldeneyes, a kind of mountain sunflower, are beset by buprestid beetles. In some lights these small oblong insects are iridescent green, in others gold or bronze. Heather and I can hardly dislodge them from their feast of petals and pollen. They sparkle in rainbow colors, alight with a thousand tiny prisms. White-throated swifts, one or two at a time, swoosh overhead, silent except for the rush of air through their wings. A bumblebee plops onto a geranium petal, nearly bringing the flower to the ground. Normally, I'm not much of a pedagogue, but children, especially our own, bring out the teacher in all of us, and I cannot resist showing Heather marble outcrops, bee-mimicking flies, and white-breasted nuthatches. When I point out the bushtits, she laughs aloud. "Bird names crack me up," she says.

Along the first mile of trail, young horned lizards are too numerous to count. Most are about the size of a quarter and can hardly be more than a few weeks old. Their heads, not yet armored with the fierce, backward pointing spines characteristic of their kind, are as bald and vulnerable as a baby's skull. Their pebbly beige and pink coloring conceal them so well that we fail to see them until they scamper out from underfoot. Like many other montane lizards, they are born alive at a time of year when abundant food—ants in this case—allows them to grow quickly before the winter comes. Heather coos over the babies, of course, but is not quite quick enough to catch one. When she spies a somnolent adult, she bends down and strokes its back. The lizard whips its head around and hisses audibly, mouth wide open. Suitably reproved, we go on our way.

As always in the autumn, oak galls are plentiful and varied. Glued to the undersides of oak leaves, some look like miniature peaches, others like mistletoe berries. "But what is it, exactly?" she asks when I point out a third type of gall, a creamy sphere bristling with maroon spines. I explain that galls are the result of interaction between the leaf and the DNA of a female wasp or fly. The gall forms when the insect inserts her eggs between the inner and outer layers of the leaf. The leaf provides the raw materials for the gall; the wasp's DNA controls what form those materials will take.

As Heather listens and nods, I wonder why we have not done this more often. Time slipped away, somehow, and soon she will slip away too.

Even now she is speculating about finding an apartment close to work and not too far from a grocery store. Until winter, when she will rely on buses, she'll get around the city by bicycle. "I hope my bike isn't delayed in shipping," she says.

Steve, meanwhile, has been considering the sturdy stalk of a dead agave as a potential walking stick. Now he announces that carpenter bees have nested in it. Through a dime-sized hole in the epidermis, we can see into the hollow center of the stalk. The nest, such as it is, has been long abandoned. Steve says that we will find occupied nests only in standing agave stalks, those still filled with pith and heavy with fluids. I realize then that the reason I have never found a carpenter bee nest is that I never knew to look in standing stalks.

Much of nature study lies in knowing what to look for, and it is a lucky child who has someone to point these things out. Camped along the California coast several years ago, Steve and I watched a group of twelve-year-olds follow a pretty woman in her twenties through a campground. The woman carried a clipboard, and every child was equipped with notebook and pencil. They walked slowly, stopped often. "A nature walk," Steve said, and so it seemed to be. We overheard the woman talking about bracken fern, how the tips of the youngest fronds, called fiddleheads, can be broken off and eaten. They taste like almonds, she said, but contain arsenic, so moderation is advised. One boy, lagging behind the others, scribbled furiously in his notebook. I imagined him writing, "Fiddleheads, moderation advised," and told Steve, "That kid is going to be a biologist someday."

A bumblebee worries around and around us as if trying to figure out the geometry of these three inexplicable flowers. Heather regards it calmly. She must have learned this from me, not her father, who is leery of bees, wasps, and all stinging things. But where did she learn to love hiking? All through childhood, she accompanied us only with the greatest reluctance. "Oh, Mom, do I have to?" she would plead. What response can a parent make to that? Yes, you *have* to come out and enjoy nature? Once she became a teenager, she steadfastly refused to go along. Hiking was too dirty, too sweaty, and too effortful to arouse her interest.

We stop to rest on a rocky promontory. Millions of lady beetles have stopped here, too. They paint the tree trunks red and fill every crevice in the outcrop. Heather lets them crawl onto her fingertips, then holds them in the air until they fly away.

Ambling ahead of us, Steve discovers a rattlesnake stretched out across the path. Locating snakes is one of his talents. He could probably find them on Antarctica or Mars. This one is an Arizona black, a beautiful, glossy snake patterned like a fishnet stocking in black and gold. The snake shows no inclination to move, so Steve stirs it up with a stick. Instantly, it coils and rattles, then slides off the trail, still rattling. We watch as it twines into the lower branches of a manzanita. Its sinuous upper body, lapped back and forth on itself, hangs in the air like a rope trick while the black tongue flicks and quivers. Not for a second does it cease rattling.

Steve asks, "Do you have your tape recorder?"

Sometimes I carry a pocket-sized tape recorder with me instead of a notebook. I hand it to him, and he gets down on his hands and knees and holds it out toward the snake.

"What in the world are you trying to do?"

"Get the rattle on tape."

He has no luck. Playing the tape as we head back up the trail, what we hear is my plaintive voice nagging him not to get so close.

I snip off a sprig of white phlox—*Linanthastrum nuttallii*. Different populations of this species have distinct odors. The fragrance is always sweet yet generally has some unusual undertone—sometimes lemony, sometimes musky. These smell exactly like maple syrup— or, rather, exactly like maple syrup tastes. "What do you suppose is the selective advantage of smelling like maple syrup?" I ask, but Steve and Heather have fallen behind and cannot hear me.

They stopped to examine some bear scat, he explains when they catch up. At this time of year, when the bears are fattening themselves for hibernation on manzanita berries and acorns, their scat is often as dry and crumbly as a handful of granola. "I hadn't realized bears ate so many acorns," Steve says, "but it stands to reason."

"If you were lost out here, could you survive by eating off the land for a couple of weeks?" Heather asks.

"No way," Steve and I say in unison.

"There's nothing to eat," I add.

"Well, what *would* you do?"

Steve says, "You'd have to do what the bears do. Dig for grubs."

She makes a face, and I too wonder whether I could bring myself to eat grubs. We speculate about other possibilities as we walk up the trail. You could eat wild mushrooms, assuming you knew which were edible, but they would not have much food value. And in the autumn there would be acorns, as long as you knew how to remove the tannins. I mention Cabeza de Vaca, the sixteenth-century Spanish explorer who, shipwrecked off the coast of Florida, painfully and slowly forged a route across the Southwest to the coast of California. Along the way he met many different Indian tribes, and most were starving. One group depended almost entirely on prickly pear fruits for sustenance, and in the months when the fruits were not available, they became weak and haggard. "And these were hunter-gatherers," I remind Heather, "people who specialized in living off the land, not city softies like us."

"Better not to get lost in the first place," is her conclusion.

Fallen acorns, some capped, some not, pebble the ground. The tiny caps are a tight squeeze on my fingertip. As a child, I would have filled all my pockets with acorns, then stuffed the overflow into my father's. My parents were not biologists, not even nature lovers in the conventional way; yet somehow they conveyed a sense of the out-of-doors as precious and special. Given half a chance, nature can do the job almost by itself. What child would not be captivated by baby horned lizards and acorn caps and agave leaves as stuffed with lady beetles as a celery stalk with peanut butter? One way or the other, we must teach our children well lest all the conservation measures undertaken by one generation be emasculated by the next.

Buckbrush is in full bloom today. Multitudes of winged insects nectar at the small, white blossoms. As we brush past, the insects rise slightly into the air, then settle back immediately. Many are marina blues, small butterflies that disappear when they perch with wings folded. Their silver underwings are as good as an invisible cape, and when they fly, they leap into existence with a flash of periwinkle blue.

As I stop to watch a nuthatch pricking insects from ponderosa pine bark, Steve and Heather stroll ahead. Their voices drift back along the trail. For a moment, caught up entirely in the natural world, she has forgotten all the commotion and anxiety of getting ready to leave. (Our gift to her.)

# 16

## walking through memory

I'm glad for my sweater on this early October morning, especially when the sun slips behind the clouds. The aspens are turning, the leaves yellow, freckled with brown. Falling, they catch in the splayed branches of the Douglas firs. Last week Heather sent me an envelope from Pittsburgh filled with autumn leaves that she had collected and pressed. When I slit it open, maple, oak, catalpa, sycamore, and liquidambar tumbled out and spilled across the table.

Her letter said, "I wish I had a camera so I could photograph the gorgeous oranges, yellows, reds, and browns that have invaded the city. I'd say that about half the trees are consumed with every color *but* green. Although I really miss the Southwest, I love this newfound experience that is autumn."

How hard we fight to define ourselves as different from our parents, only to come back to what we were taught in the first place. The lesson sinks in, it seems, even if parents don't always know that they are teaching.

Aspen leaves crackle underfoot, patter on the trees With every gust of wind, another handful of leaves flies before us like yellow butterflies. One leaf turns over and over along the trail before it cartwheels between the blades of a sedge, where it is pinned fast.

"Finally it feels like autumn to me," Steve says. "Sure seems like this summer has gone fast." He sounds a little melancholy. Time moves faster as we grow older, I remind him. Small comfort. I too find autumn a sadder and sadder season every year even though I recognize the necessity of it: a signal that change is on the way, a time for plants and animals to wind down, to prepare for winter.

A pleasant sense of anticipation soon whisks our blues away. The trail down Lefthand Canyon is a new one for us, and anything could happen. Quite soon, anything does. Steve's feet launch themselves into the air, then follow him with a thump as he comes back down unhurt on his butt and elbows.

"What in the hell was that?" he asks. We examine the spot where his feet left the ground and find a bunch of hailstones hidden by fallen leaves. The likeliest source of the hail was a thunderstorm late yesterday afternoon. Given that the hailstones are almost as big as marbles now, I am glad that we were not around to accept delivery. Elsewhere, sunshine has melted the hail, making the perfect set-up for Mother Nature's little booby trap. With our sense of anticipation both justified and whetted, we continue down the trail.

After half a mile, we realize that this trail has been abandoned. If foot traffic were more frequent, the path would be bare, but here rosettes of daisy, geranium, and strawberry make a solid mat down the center. Whatever water bars existed are long since gone. Water bars are logs or rocks that divert running water off the trail. Instead of water bars, fallen trees, well rotted and overgrown with moss, make great hummocks across the trail like bears hidden under carpets. The blazes are mostly gone, too. Blazing—making a rectangular cut in a tree trunk at eye level—was once a popular way of marking trails. When marked trees fall, they take their blazes with them, and that is what has happened here.

"How many people do you think we'll see today?" Steve asks. His little joke. We could well be the first people to walk this trail in a year.

I used to blame the Forest Service for allowing our trails, mostly constructed by the Civilian Conservation Corps during the depression, to fall into disrepair. Either the government lacked funds for trail maintenance, I figured, or it preferred to spend its dollars in other ways. Now I wonder if trails are not being abandoned by the very people who should be using them. In the Pinaleños, Santa Ritas, Rincons, Santa Catalinas, and Huachucas, Steve and I meet other people only when we take the most popular hikes. These are very popular indeed, and on a summer day, we might see a dozen people along the Miller Peak Trail in the Huachuca Mountains or twice that many on the Marshall Gulch Loop in the Santa Catalinas. Meanwhile, forest quietly reclaims the Lefthand Canyon Trail. Evidently the more a trail is ignored, the more forbidding it appears, and, in an inevitable cycle of desuetude, the more likely it is to be ignored in the future.

Aspen saplings whip against our legs. In some places, the trail is overgrown with prickly thickets of raspberry, locust, and gooseberry—*Rubus, Robinia,* and *Ribes,* the three R's. I can discern something of a footpath beneath the thicket, so I hack my way through, glad that I'm wearing long sleeves and pants. Once a trail has been abandoned, the last thing to go is the level line where thousands of feet have walked—the treadway, it is called. Even covered by leaves or colonized by raspberry bushes, the treadway remains, a sure sign that humans passed this way at one time.

I remember the time when Heather and I went backpacking in Paria Canyon, a narrow gulch that straddles the border between southern Utah and northern Arizona. To her surprise, the stream bed was the trail, and we often walked in water. The absence of a well-trodden path made her wonder aloud how often you must walk over a place before it becomes a path.

"I don't know," I said. "It probably depends on the terrain." In the desert, where soil is a thin and fragile construction of prehistoric origin, maybe once or twice. In a forest, where rotting leaves and needles spring back to obliterate your passage, maybe a dozen times or more.

As she and I walked, I began to imagine a time when there were neither paths nor human feet to follow them. I pictured an untrampled, untrodden Earth, an enormous globe where unparted grasses swayed shoulder-high, the forest wall showed no break, and rippled sand displayed only the imprints of rain drops and beetle claws. Floating above the curved surface of the planet, I noticed that the only clearly delineated routes were the wavering blue channels where rivers and streams cut their own paths, and, far up in the mountains, where the wide white tongues of glaciers rasped out icy highways.

Perhaps it *was* like this once, but I doubt it. Something in the brain leads to path making, and not in the human brain alone. Wild mice make and follow foraging routes. Migrating birds follow invisible flight paths. Even harvester ants trace the same paths again and again until the terrain around their nest looks like a wagon wheel. What is the brain, after all, but a pathway prototype, an immensely complicated network created by chemicals and electricity flowing from here to there? And so the primeval Earth must have been marked by paths—the paths of butterflies seeking refuge from winter cold; the paths of ants trundling grains of soil one way, grains of seed another; the paths of lizards feeding upon the ants.

Following old, long-abandoned trails, I have an eerie sense of the trail itself as something human, or nearly so. As the treadway vanishes under overhanging branches, I glimpse my route in fits and starts. It is a dotted line that my feet follow unerringly even when my eyes cannot. My feet, understanding the logic of the path, seldom fail to turn the corner at a switchback. As long as the treadway exists, my feet cleave to it as if following a path is what they were meant for. Sometimes the path is so well hidden by overhanging plants that I place my feet with nothing but faith to guide them. I can reason out these faded routes if I want (well, the leaves seem more heavily trodden here, while the branches there are interlocking and I'd have to force my way through), but my subconscious mind accomplishes the same process almost instantaneously, so that my feet are following the treadway before my mind has decided which way to turn.

A red-tailed hawk flies overhead, perches on the topmost branch of a tall snag. Through binoculars, I see a brown head and dark brown wings mottled with gold. Except for a brown necklace, the breast is porcelain white. As it sits there, turning its head back and forth, there's a sudden paucity of birdlife in the vicinity. Evidently I'm not the only one to notice the hawk's arrival.

This reach of Lefthand Canyon burned some time ago. The oldest Douglas firs, the ones with the thickest bark, withstood the fire. Their trunks are blackened near the base but otherwise undamaged. Younger trees were killed but not consumed. Some still stand, a toothpick forest. Many have fallen, and the forest floor resembles a beach after a bad winter storm. In some places polished, gray logs lie side by side as if to make a corduroy road. Elsewhere they are toppled like pickup sticks dumped out of the can. If not for the trail, we would have a hard time making our way over the deadfall. Even with the trail, progress is slow: it has been some time since the last forest ranger came along with chain saw and hatchet, and the route is often barred by massive fallen logs.

Slow progress is not necessarily bad. It forces us to pay attention to the trail, what is left of it. Little-used trails call for extra caution unless you want to get lost. Steve and I did get lost once, on a trail much like this one. It happened on a backpacking trip in the Gila Wilderness of southwestern New Mexico. The faintness of that trail should have been fair warning, but we had always prided ourselves on our ability to follow any man-made path, no matter how vague.

I remember that as the trail filed into the bottom of Dry Canyon, it became obscured by fallen trees too large to clamber over. We skirted the deadfalls as best we could, returning always to the trail, a feat that became increasingly problematic as the trail became fainter and fainter. Eventually, there was nothing to return to. The treadway had simply petered out. When we looked back in the direction from which we came, we could not reconstruct our route. The trail had disappeared in both directions, leaving no obvious path through the forest. Consulting one another and the map, we decided to follow the stream down the canyon to its junction with another trail. Feeling some anxiety, we pushed on at a rapid rate, as rapid as thickets of dogwood and nettle would allow. At regular intervals, cliffs and waterfalls forced us to bushwhack up the steep side slope, then back down. Each time, this maneuver became harder than the last as we grew more and more exhausted. There was never a secure place for our feet: fir cones, pine needles, oak leaves, rocks, bark, everything was poised to slide as soon as we stepped on it. We hauled ourselves up the slope by grasping clumps of grass or small trees. Once, a sizable slab of rock slid out from under me, and I would have tumbled backward all the way to the canyon bottom but for my grip on a sturdy fir sapling.

Steve kept ahead of me much of the time, pioneering our route. Every so often, he stopped, looked back, called, "How are you doing?" I caught up with him at last on a rocky promontory. He was looking downstream. I will never forget that moment. Under other circumstances, it would have been spectacular scenery. Below us, the canyon bottom pinched out between immense polished boulders; we could hear but not see a pounding waterfall. Above us stretched a long scree slope capped by fantastically jagged cliffs. And directly ahead, a tilted rock slab ended in a fifty-foot drop. A nervy hiker might have been able to cross it, but we could not. We were cliffed out.

That is when I realized we were in trouble. We were not lost, because we knew our approximate location, nor were we confused or disoriented. But . . . But having abandoned the abandoned trail, we were not certain we could find it again. Worried, exhausted, embarrassed, Steve said, "I had no idea how easy it is to get lost."

Clearly, our only reasonable alternative was to backtrack. And so we did, plunging down the slope we had so laboriously inched up. We returned to a campsite that Steve had dismissed three hours earlier as "barely adequate" and set up our tent and sleeping bags in the last half hour of daylight.

That night my mind kept circling through the same incidents and fears, like a dog hunting for a scent. Over and over I rehearsed the events of the day. Over and over I wondered what would happen if we couldn't find the trail out. Would we be able to signal an airplane? How long would our food last?

As maybe once or twice before in my life, I pleaded with a higher power to save us. I made no bargains; I simply prayed. I thought of my friend Barbara and her canoeing trip on the Cumberland River. She and her companion had wrecked the canoe, lost most of their food and clothing, and yet they had survived. I remembered my friend George and why he prefers kayaking to rafting: "I like to feel the power of the river," he says. And I knew that what I was feeling at that moment was the power of the wilderness. "Isn't this why you came here?" I asked myself, and while the answer was certainly not an emphatic "Yes," it wasn't exactly a "No" either.

At last I put myself to sleep by imagining the rooms in the house where I had grown up. How well I still knew every room and its contents. Memory was made keen by absence, I suppose, since my parents had long since moved to another state. I recalled, one by one, the books in the living room bookcase: *Audubon's Birds, Bullfinch's Mythology, Treasure Island,* and *Kidnapped.* I pictured the linoleum tiles in the bathroom, the hallway linen cupboard, the big round kitchen table, and the blue upholstered chairs in the living room.

After I fell asleep, I dreamed about finding a wrapper from a candy bar, bright and crisp, and I knew that someone else had preceded us quite recently. This seemed comforting. I awoke toward morning and understood that everything would be all right.

And it was. After a sketchy breakfast, Steve led us to the lost trail as though he had been practicing for that moment all his life.


Somewhere I read the following statement: "I used to think of the trail as my lifeline." The author implied that she had grown beyond all that, and perhaps she had. Not me. Ever since that trip, I have known that trails *are* my lifeline. More than that, they are my foot line, my mind line, my heart line.

No matter where I am, the trail I travel now connects me to all the trails I've ever traveled and to every trail I will travel in the future. Walking in the Gila Wilderness another time, Steve and I found wild roses in flower, and I remembered how my daughter first inhaled that intensely sweet and cinnamony fragrance when she and I were backpacking in Paria Canyon. "Heather waited twenty-one years to smell this," I told Steve, snipping off a single flower with my thumb-nail. Later, when he startled a female grouse, then nearly stepped on one of her chicks that was huddled in the trail like a clump of dried leaves, I remembered the grouse with young we had seen many years before in southern Utah. That time, a half-dozen chicks had exploded from underfoot like billiard balls scattered with a cue stick. Long after we passed, we could hear the anxious mother clucking and cooing as she reassembled her family.

Walking on trails, walking through memory, I realize that places are natural containers for memory. In fact, memory itself is a place, as Edward Casey points out, "a place wherein the past can revive and survive; it is a place for places." If we move, what I lose is the chance to experience this place immediately, and that is sad. That is indeed a considerable loss. But I get to keep all my past experiences of it. I can revisit it in memory anytime I like.

After passing through a long shaft of sunlight, I come to a place where Douglas firs cast dense shade across the trail. I pause and look ahead to where sunshine slants down through the forest canopy, illuminating the green wall. The sheen of needles looks like spider gossamer, a sheet of gossamer gleaming in the sun. An aspen trunk creaks in the wind. Small birds utter sweet, entangled notes. I walk back into the sunshine, out of shadow into light, out of coolness into warmth. As the sun's face warms mine, contentment permeates my bones.

What animals we are at bottom, as Barbara says. I realize now that I walk for sanity. I walk for joy. I walk to be most fully human, and it is trails that take me there.

# 17 writing the future

The trail to Miller Peak, the highest point in the Huachuca Mountains, is supposedly a mere five miles long. It seems more like ten miles, and I strongly suspect that the official distance was measured on a creased and wrinkled map. The moment we arrive on the summit, I collapse in a heap, too exhausted to seek protection from the brisk October wind. It is a good five minutes, in fact, before I even have the energy to slough off my pack. Steve, irritatingly chipper, strolls here and there listing plants in his field notebook, occasionally picking some plant and stuffing it into the plastic bag in which we accumulate our finds. Although certain that he is making dozens of marvelous botanical discoveries that should be mine, I am too tired to do anything about it.

We hoped that we would have Miller Peak to ourselves, but a man and woman in their early twenties have already claimed it. Across the rocks they have spread a virtual commissary, including briquettes, lighter fluid, a barbecue grill, a pink tablecloth, and a styrofoam cooler packed with ice and canned soft drinks. It has been quite a while since I wanted to impress anyone that badly. As the woman pulls silverware and plates from her pack, the man starts to build a charcoal fire. From bits of conversation, I gather that they will be cooking shrimp and corn on the cob. Comparing my menu— the usual crackers, cheese, and grapes—with theirs, I briefly consider throwing myself on their mercy, but Steve forestalls me by return- ing with the news that he has found *Agoseris arizonica*. Not only is it an uncommon wildflower in southern Arizona, he points out, it is also a new species for our flora.

The *Agoseris* brings the total number of species known from the Huachuca Mountains to 890, roughly 10 percent larger than the pre- liminary list we made two years ago. The first list was based on speci- mens collected during the past ninety years by the dozens of bota- nists who preceded us. Thanks to their efforts, the flora was fairly well known before we started our project. Our contribution will be the adding of nearly one hundred species and, more importantly, the publishing of an up-to-date list. In the beginning, our list grew by leaps and bounds. Now, after several dozen collecting trips, each suc- cessive hike adds fewer species, thereby intensifying the competition in our largely one-sided rivalry.

As long as our final list is relatively complete, length per se is more or less irrelevant. A flora of one thousand species is not twice as good as a flora half that large. The number of species in a given place de- pends on many factors, among them geographic location, areal ex- tent, topographic relief, variety of rock types, and presence or ab- sence of permanent water. Because these factors are constrained in one way or another, the size of any flora is constrained as well. If the limits of the Huachuca Mountains flora are finite, we should be able to enumerate every species, yet we know from practice that our list will fall short of definitive completeness. We are only human, for one thing, and from carelessness, ignorance, or sheer inattention, we will inevitably overlook some species and no doubt misidentify others. Moreover, we are only two people, and we cannot explore every canyon, ridge, peak, and spring in every month of the growing season. Plant lists for large areas such as the Huachuca Mountains are at best a sample of the actual flora. When we reach a point of greatly diminished returns, we will declare the project done, content in the knowledge that we sampled as many combinations of habitat and season as possible.

As we eat lunch, I unfold a topographic map of the Huachuca Mountains for the peculiar pleasure of matching document to landscape. Paul Simon tells us in a song that everyone loves the sound of distant trains, a universal pleasure, or so we all believe. In the same way, we all love maps, only each person believes that it is a unique and private pleasure shared by no more than a discerning few. "I *love* maps," people have confessed to me as though owning up to some odd but rather splendid trait—a yen for Antarctic travel, perhaps, or a fondness for larks'-tongues.

For years I took the appropriate topographic maps on all my hikes but seldom examined them. Like the windproof, waterproof matches I kept in a metal match safe, they were mostly for use in case of emergency, an outcome that my natural caution made exceedingly unlikely. When minor emergencies did arise, maps failed me more often than not—or, more truthfully, I failed them. I remember my puzzlement when Heather and I were in Paria Canyon where sheer, vertical walls sealed us off from a wider view of mountains, knolls, or other landmarks. Examining our map, I felt as if we had stumbled through Alice's looking glass into an inverse dimension. The map, omniscient and serene, gazed down at our narrow world from a bird's-eye view, while we, wormlike and confused, peered up from below. Nothing in the landscape seemed to match the lines printed on paper, and after a while I simply gave up trying to read the map. Having only two ways to go—upstream or down—we were hardly in danger of getting lost in any case.

Nowadays, believing with James Davidson and John Rugge that

adventure is a sign of poor planning, I no longer reserve maps for emergencies. I especially like to whip out a map when I am high in the mountains with a fine view in every direction, because it is then that the map and I share exactly the same perspective on the landscape, both of us on top looking down. Sometimes I can almost hear the tumblers in my brain clicking into place as features on the landscape interlock with their counterparts on paper. The intensity of my satisfaction at those moments suggests that reading maps can be something more than an intellectual exercise.

Surveying the landscape from Miller Peak, I get an inkling of what that something might be, as memories, and memories of memories, enrich the view. Sutherland Peak lies about two miles to the west, and I remember a time when Steve and I camped near the peak and used a map and compass to pick out Miller Peak from the array of prominent points on the ridgeline above us. Now I am fascinated to see from the back side a landscape we studied from the front, fascinated as well to follow with my eyes the trails we have traced with our feet.

In unfamiliar territory, a person can of course find her way without maps, if she can read the landscape. That kind of literacy demands long experience in the out-of-doors. I think here of John Bigelow, a lieutenant in the United States Army who spent part of his career chasing Apaches along the Arizona–Mexico border. From the little I have read, he seems to have been level-headed, curious, and intelligent. In 1885, Bigelow climbed to the top of the Huachuca Mountains and reported afterwards that he had learned more about the topography of southern Arizona and Sonora in ten minutes of gazing than he could have picked up in ten weeks of scouting. In his report, he listed the mountain ranges he could see: the Chiricahuas, Dragoons, Galiuros, Santa Ritas, Patagonias, Mules, and others; he must have recognized them from days and weeks of sometimes dangerous and often tedious reconnaissance on the ground. I gather that he was a brave man, too. And a romantic one: he said that as long and intently as he stared, he could not look his fill.

In reading landscapes, as in many other endeavors, a proper set of terms is indispensable, like the !Kung with their acacia thicket near the slope beside the baobab tree. English–speaking geomorphologists have assembled a technical vocabulary rich in borrowed words for landscape features. Many of these words were originally folk terms, such as the German words *felsenmeer*, or "sea of rock," for boulder fields, and *inselberg*, or "island mountain," for the erosion–resistant knolls left behind as a mountain front retreats. From French, geomorphologists have borrowed *cirque* to mean a mountain–slope hollow created by glacial scouring and erosion. Arabic, well furnished with words for sandy landscapes, has supplied *barchan* and *seif* for particular types of dunes. In one way or another, we find the words we need for thinking or speaking about the land on which we live.

We even find words that encompass *those* words: geography, cartography, topography. Earth writing, map writing, landscape writing. Contemplating these words, I envision the landscape as a huge inscription by an unseen hand, a text I can clamber up, slide down, and stumble across, a world of knowledge to be apprehended as much with limbs, heart, and lungs as with eyes, ears, and brain. That is how you eventually come to know a piece of land—not from photographs or descriptions or even maps, but from investing yourself in it and on it, taking risks and making a commitment as you do to marriage or medical school or even to compiling a flora.

The willingness to encounter risk and the capacity for commitment tend to be associated with opposite ends of the age spectrum, which is why collectors and compilers—whether of birds, plants, minerals, or mollusks—are most productive of specimens when they are young and of knowledge when they are old. For our knowledge of the Huachuca Mountains flora as it was ninety years ago, Steve and I are greatly indebted to an apparently tireless young man named Leslie Goodding, who was a high school teacher in the mining town of Bisbee about thirty–five miles to the east. Later in his life he became a range scientist, and later still he wrote a newspaper column entitled "Chats about Plants." Conveniently for us, Goodding not only collected hundreds of specimens in the Huachuca Mountains, but he also had the foresight to deposit most of them in the university herbarium, where we eventually utilized them as a kind of communal memory.

Without Goodding's specimens, for instance, Steve and I would never have known that wild rose grew on Carr Peak in 1909, because in our trips up, down, and around the peak, we have found no wild roses at all. By comparing recent collections with those preserved in the communal memory of the herbarium, we infer that other species are missing, too, about thirty altogether. All were collected in the Huachuca Mountains before 1960; none has been collected there since. No doubt a few still grow somewhere in the range, and with luck we will stumble across them eventually. We are convinced that many others, however, have truly disappeared, victims of forest fires, droughts, floods, grazing, and housing developments. All the missing species grow elsewhere in Arizona or Mexico; we cannot, thank heavens, call them extinct. We can, however, provisionally consider them as having been extirpated from the Huachuca Mountains.

One hundred years from now, a different pair of botanists can assess new gains and losses in the Huachuca flora by using our list and specimens as a baseline. Their results, amending and amplifying ours, will both justify the work we do now and secure our place in the communal memory.


Steve looks at his watch and suggests that it is time to go. I am reluctant to leave; like Bigelow, I cannot look my fill. The gray ramparts of Huachuca Peak to the north remind me of our first hike to the summit when a frenzied rustling in the undergrowth burst forth in the shape of a fawn. Except for its spots and its erect, white tail, the fawn was as red as a fox and about the same size. It shot across a clearing and disappeared into dense brush so fast that at first we thought it was a fox. When lunchtime came, we sat gingerly at the edge of Huachuca Peak, legs dangling. Just beyond our toes, mats of rock rose clung to the limestone cliff. Steve had brought a can of sardines for his lunch, but the lid was defective and could not be unsealed. He hacked at it with his Swiss army knife, employing every blade and implement except the toothpick, until, infuriated beyond endurance, he jumped up, cocked his arm, and hurled the can into oblivion.

I suppose the can and its contents still lie on the saddle below Huachuca Peak unless some enterprising bear has obtained and learned to operate a can opener. Steve takes my hands and hauls me to my feet. I stare a final time to the west, where the San Rafael Valley is a golden plain feathered with green watercourses. To the east, where we are headed, the San Pedro Valley is gridded with roads and subdivisions. Lieutenant Bigelow noticed a similar contrast. "On the American side of the line," he reported, "could be seen roads and houses and settlements—not many, but enough to suggest a prosperous and growing population." No roads were to be seen on the Mexican side of the border, which he described as "dreary and weird."

Bigelow's destiny was caught up with that of his nation in a way that mine is not, nor is it ever likely to be. Scouting the rugged borderlands and scrambling up and down the Huachuca Mountains, he was writing the landscape, writing the earth, writing the future of his country. His life appears as grand and huge as a Titian in comparison to the miniature Dürer of my own life. As much as I admire Bigelow's outdoorsmanship, however, I am separated from him by gender, occupation, and more than one hundred years of history, and I must disagree with his assessment of the view: for me it is the sparsely settled land to the west and south that is beautiful, not the prosperous plains to the north and east. Even so, I cannot—must not—forget that the future Bigelow wrote made it possible for me to be here now. As ever, our future arises from our past, knowledge that somehow gives me hope.

# *18* fear falls away

Throughout the wet November night I have been aware of the hard knot of fear that has been lodged in my throat for ten days now, ever since Renée invited me to accompany her and three others in climbing Baboquivari Peak.

"I'd love to," I said, whereupon my throat tied itself into a knot. The other major peaks in southeastern Arizona are accessible by trails, and anyone with strong legs and lungs can hike to the summits. Only Baboquivari requires more: ropes, harness, and carabiners if you have them, or better-than-average climbing skills and plenty of confidence if you do not. I have a harness, a carabiner, and not much else except Renée's assurance that I can make the climb. The route we will use is rated class four, so it is not a technical climb— the holds being large enough that ropes are not absolutely necessary. On the other hand, a class four rating also indicates enough exposure to kill or maim you if you fall. Renée promised that she and

Gordon, her husband, would bring their climbing equipment. This would have set my mind at ease if she had not emphasized *bring*, leaving me with the impression that she would prefer not to use the equipment at all. For a whole week, I have been promising myself that if I just do this one climb, I will never have to climb again. I've lost track of the number of times I have asked Renée if she is absolutely positive that I can do it. Am I secretly hoping she will change her mind?

Of the five of us, only Kirk has no experience with rocks and ropes. Gordon has been climbing since he was a boy and could manipulate the equipment in his sleep. Renée is also a good and fearless climber. Gordon and Renée have ascended Baboquivari Peak several times by the Forbes route, the one we will use today. Laurie, strong and graceful on rocks, has enough confidence to climb anything. Knowing that I could hardly be in better hands brings no comfort. People have died on this route. People have also started and been turned back by incapacity or fear. I knew two women twenty years ago who began the climb with their husbands in expectation of an easy scramble. When the women became terrified and wanted to turn back, the men refused. My friends survived, no mean accomplishment, but what remained in their minds was the fear, not the triumph.

Even if I had never heard that particular story, I would still be scared. My fear of heights is exceeded in my experience only by my husband's fear: I am decidedly nervous when I am less than two feet away from a precipice; standing another two feet behind me, Steve will be outspokenly anxious on both our behalves, and only when we retreat to a safer distance will he relax. Like my friends of twenty years ago, I have experienced uncontrollable fear in the midst of a climb; like them, I have been unable to move and certain of death. I too survived, but it felt like failure.

Despite these and other truly excellent reasons for staying at home with a good book, or even a bad one, here I am. Years ago, when I half believed in astral travel and other occult nonsense, I read somewhere that not only is Baboquivari Peak sacred to the Tohono O'odham, it is also a "power point" such as Carlos Castaneda describes in his *Don Juan* books. Castaneda's work has been exposed as fictional, if not fraudulent, but the idea that Baboquivari Peak is a sacred and powerful place transcends scholarly criteria for verifiable truths. The desire to be on Baboquivari Peak, born at the moment I read those words, has never left me and is one reason I am here. Unlike other sacred peaks in our area, Baboquivari looks like a holy mountain. A 1,500-foot-tall granite dome rising from an otherwise unremarkable ridgeline, Baboquivari Peak resembles a bishop's miter tossed on a rumpled robe. It can be identified from a hundred miles away, and when I am high in the mountains, I never fail to look for it. Always I have looked, then shifted my glance, all too willing to accept Baboquivari Peak as my Impossible Dream. Now the prospect of moving away, combined with Renée's fortuitous invitation, makes it clear that if I do not tilt at that windmill today, I never will.

Apparently no one slept very well last night. To call us *subdued* this morning would be to greatly overestimate the average level of cheeriness. The ground is still wet from rain, and the log where we sat at suppertime is sodden. Breakfast is a dismal meal eaten under dreary skies. Gordon and Renée talk quietly together in one part of camp, Laurie and Kirk in another. I sit on an uncomfortable rock by myself and sip coffee from a plastic mug. My free hand, shoved into a jacket pocket, fingers a metal bottle cap that I have brought on purpose. Long ago someone told me that if you throw a bottle cap off the peak, the cap falls up instead of down because wind currents snatch it away. Dubious but hopeful, I am prepared. Maybe that is the real reason I have come—to fling a bottle cap from Baboquivari Peak.

Eventually, a spattering of rain stirs us to pack our belongings. There is some laconic talk of what to do in case it really rains. Wait out the storm in a rock shelter? Cancel the climb? In my head I am shouting, "Cancel! Cancel!" but I suspect that only a hurricane could allow me to back out at this point without losing face. Immersed in my own pitiful misery, I nearly miss Gordon's quiet statement that everyone will use ropes for the entire climb. My heart lifts. I might fall, but at least I will not die, probably will not even be maimed. Bless the man. I will love him forever.


We camped last night within easy striking distance of the peak, so we have only a short hike this morning. This side of the Baboquivari Mountains—the west side—belongs to the Tohono O'odham Nation. Renée and Gordon obtained permission for our climb ahead of time; most people use the eastern approach to save themselves the bother of getting a permit. As we walk, a blue umbrella unfurls overhead, rolling the clouds to the perimeter of the sky. We talk of this and that, including how the Forbes route was established. Georgie Scott, the young woman who eventually became Mrs. Forbes, had so many suitors that she could not decide among them. ("Oh, poor thing," Renée interjects.) Like a princess in a fairy tale, Georgie set a challenge: the first suitor to climb to the top of Baboquivari Peak, something no Anglo had ever done, would be the one she married. Robert Forbes made three attempts before he finally discovered a feasible route in 1898. It required creeping up the Great Ramp, a vast granite slab, then scaling an eighty-foot vertical pitch that had decent holds unless you strayed off line. Above that pitch, you had an easy scramble to the top. It was nightfall by the time Forbes completed his first successful ascent. Elated, he lit a bonfire that could be seen as far away as Tucson. Georgie might have been the only person to know the fire for what it was. Everyone else thought that Baboquivari Peak was erupting.

Our trail parallels the crest of the range, ducking under small, gnarled oaks and skirting boldly colored outcrops shaped like prehistoric beasts. These rocks are not the smooth, hard granite of the peak itself but a crumbly volcanic tuff in hues of tan, rusty orange, and maroon. Gray twists of coyote scat are plentiful on the trail, crumbled bear dung not uncommon. The abundance of wild animal sign suggests a place not much used by humans or, better still, one used in ways that create little disruption.

Much sooner than I like, we arrive at the Great Ramp. It tilts up-ward at just enough of an angle to make my palms sweat. We step into our climbing harnesses, which basically comprise two adjust-able thigh loops connected front and back to an adjustable waist loop. My harness, garishly striped with pink and yellow, elicits the usual comments—"if the rope breaks, at least you'll be easy to see at the bottom of the cliff," and so forth. Gordon and Renée flake out the ropes, feeding them length by length from neat coils into loose, lazy loops on the ground. I pick up a rope and, about three feet from the end, tie a knot that looks like the number eight. I thread the end of the rope through my harness, leaving the knot dangling, then loop the end back to the knot. Next, by coaxing the end of the rope through the knot, following every twist and turn, I create an iden-tical figure eight that hugs the original knot. This ingenious two-phase device links my harness (and therefore me) to the climbing system so securely that it will be hard to untie when the climb is over. Finally, I secure the loose end with half a double fisherman, which is a double fisherman tied once. Don't ask me why it is not simply called *a fisherman.*

I check to make sure that my knots are properly tied. Renée checks my knots, and I check hers. Gordon checks my knots and double-checks his own. Laurie checks my knots and Kirk's. Kirk and Renée check one another's knots, then I check Kirk's, and he checks mine. All of them look fine. Clearly, none of our lives will be jeopardized by a badly tied knot today.

At last we are ready to ascend the Great Ramp. Gordon and Renée go first, then Gordon belays me, and Renée belays Kirk. Laurie is glo-riously on her own. After a minute or two of scrambling apelike with hands and feet, I realize that I could actually walk up the slab, so I do, legs a little rubbery at first, then fully in control. Midway, I look back down the slab. The base appears to drop into infinity, an un-nerving illusion; I am glad for the rope even though I do not really need it.

Above the Great Ramp, we follow a well-worn path to the vertical pitch I have been dreading. Gordon climbs first. I probably should watch every move, trying to memorize exactly where he places his hands and feet, but getting the route by rote never works for me— climbers differ greatly in strength, flexibility, and height, not to mention skill and confidence, and the holds one person uses could well be irrelevant to another's build and mind; moreover, the topography of a cliff to which you are clinging seems very different from what you saw when standing on the ground. Others climb in sequence as Gordon belays, then my turn comes. I am unpleasantly nervous until I make my first two moves, after which fear falls away, replaced by a deep interest in what I am doing. Holds arise as I need them, almost as if evoked by my need. The thick encrustations of lichen on the rock look like green snow or cucumber soup. Gray liverworts, shingled among the lichens, crunch faintly underfoot like the slender bones of birds. Aside from one tricky place where the holds become what climbers call *thin*, that is, virtually imaginary, I climb quickly and well, I feel. Renée agrees. At the top of the pitch she tells me, "You climbed that like a pro."

As advertised, the rest of the route is an easy scramble and walk. Gaining the summit is almost anticlimactic. I had expected the five of us to be crowded together like angels dancing on a pinhead; instead, the summit is flat, and broad enough for a two-bedroom house. The air is still, the sun almost hot. Renée and Laurie, having located the Tucson Mountains to the northeast, puzzle over which summit is Safford Peak. I stroll from edge to edge, grinning foolishly. I can't believe that I'm actually here. How can an Impossible Dream yield so readily to a Possible Reality? When I thank Renée for including me in the group, she says simply, "Now that you know the way, you can come back again."

Now I can remove Baboquivari Peak from my mental list of places I yearn to see at least once in my life—West Clear Creek, Aravaipa Canyon, Desolation Canyon, Mount Whitney, Keet Seel, and on and on. The list shows such a strong inclination to grow that I suspect I will never reach the end. Why it exists in the first place is not easy to explain, even to myself: it has something to do with seeing the sights that others guarantee as worthwhile, maybe, or with wanting to discover for myself the lasting appeal of some particular place.

Someone finds the trail register in a jar inside an ammo can under a small cairn. The jar holds a sheaf of paper scraps and several extremely blunt pencils. Laurie writes, "If Georgie Scott had known it would be like this, she would have climbed the peak herself." My mind goes blank, the same as it does when I must inscribe an appropriate sentiment on someone's birthday card at the office. All the time I spent fretting and worrying about the climb I could have more usefully employed in thinking up trenchant reflections for the trail register. I thumb through its pages. Many entries include praise of God and His creation. Some climbers write that they feel closer to God up here. A surprising variety of people have made the ascent: a woman five months pregnant, a group of nuns who thankfully note the assistance of "Señor Julio and his rope," a party who climbed by moonlight, reaching the summit at 2:30 A.M. Suddenly my presence here seems not such a remarkable achievement after all.

Across the Altar Valley, the Tucson and Santa Catalina mountains look like waves on a choppy sea. From past experience, I know that within a week, I will have forgotten how they look today. Within a year, I will have forgotten how it feels to be here looking at them. If I seek out new places only for the sake of accumulating sights and experiences, I might as well stop now. Yet I won't, nor would anyone else with such a list. My persistence, I suspect, has less to do with assembling a collection than it does with attempting a minor miracle: I harbor a noble but futile hope that the next climb or journey will change me for the better, or if not the next, then the one after it.

Psychological case studies demonstrate just how futile my hope is. People clutch their concepts of self as tightly as a starfish clings to a rock. A man who pictures himself as a failure is blind to whatever small successes he does achieve. A woman who has convinced herself that she is unattractive requires more than a look in the mirror to change her mind. Yet, despite our propensity to stick with the familiar, as painful as it may be, moments come when we are capable of assimilating new experience, of adapting our concepts of self to fit experience, rather than the other way around. Could it be that such moments arise most often when we let down our guard? And are we not less guarded than usual when immersed in the sights and sensations of an unfamiliar place?

Even though our favorite places offer a comfort and intimacy not to be found anywhere else, other needs lure us to unknown landscapes. Over time, the details of my climb today might slip away or even become altered in memory, but I dare to hope that being here now—and the courage it took to get here—will forever shape my attitudes and expectations. Whether I find my way back here or not, I hope that Baboquivari Peak will always be part of who I am.

# water music *19*

Late November, and killing frosts are no more than a week or two away. Only *Bidens aurea* blooms now. Every one of the yellow flowers has a blue or yellow butterfly perched upon it. When my shadow falls over them, the butterflies rise in a multicolored cloud, then settle back almost immediately, loath to let that sweetness go. There is something touching or pathetic about their anxiety for provender when the end of their lives is so near.

I jam my hands into my jacket pockets. My fingers rub the bottle cap, the one I meant to toss from Baboquivari Peak. I completely forgot about my experiment until the end of the day. By that time, we had hiked almost all the way back to the truck. I was ludicrously disappointed at first; now I think that it is just as well. Some times and places are suitable for Science; others are not and never will be.

In its lower reaches, Bear Canyon cuts into maroon and mauve conglomerate, making a shallow canyon easily entered from above via gently sloping benches. Here the canyon is shaped like a funnel, and the stream slips through bedrock sluices, forming deep, slender pools that last year–round. There are fish in these pools, and tiny snails, and a rare aquatic plant called *Lilaeopsis*. It looks like mowed grass and makes a smooth underwater turf.

Ancient sycamores arch over the stream bed. Their trunks are white, their leaves are bronze. Like cottonwoods and willows, sycamores never grow far from water. They flower early in the year and release their short-lived seeds in time for the spring runoff. If their timing is bad, or if the spring freshets fail, there will be no crop of seedlings that year. Even when seedlings do become established, they remain vulnerable for many years to scour by flash floods, trampling by cattle, and desiccation in drought. It is not uncommon to walk miles of stream bed without seeing a single sycamore under twenty feet tall.

One or two sycamore leaves at a time fall thoughtfully to the ground. The thoughtfulness comes in the rarity of the event and in the long, slow tumble from canopy to earth. Sycamores often sprout at the base, sending up long, whiplike shoots that eventually develop root systems and canopies that are independent of the parent plant. Sometimes you see rings of good-sized sycamore trees, their bases touching one another, their canopies interleaved. Probably they sprouted from a common parent that has long since died and decomposed.

Things unremarkable in themselves somehow seem well worth remarking today. We find many footprints in wet, coarse sand at the waterline—deer, raccoon, dog, human. In deep pools, slender fish shaped like willow leaves dart back and forth. Longfin dace, I think they are. Their sand–colored bodies are scarcely visible above the sandy substrate. The willow leaves on the bottom could be their yellow shadows. Sycamore leaves are plastered across the stream like water lily pads. Some are flat, some are curled; some are colored like pale suede, others like old brandy. Caught in a gentle eddy, two dozen leaves travel in a lazy circle, trailing black shadows over white rock.

Eventually they will sink to the bottom. Plenty already have, a layered mosaic of browns and golds. Sycamore leaves are tough. They last a long time in water, longer there than they do on the trees. It takes about a year for 90 percent of the leaf to be completely broken down into its constituent molecules. Light, insubstantial leaves—cottonwood, ash, and willow—take less time. The process starts rapidly as soluble compounds like sugars, amino acids, and tannins are leached out of the leaf, then slows to a crawl while the leaf is colonized by detritivores of various sorts—caddisfly larvae, snails, bacteria, and molds. This is where it all starts, really, all the vibrant aquatic life that pleases me so much—with the dropping of sycamore leaves in twos and threes onto the surface of the water.

A jumble of fist-sized cobbles has collected at the lower end of a bedrock sluice. I glance at them, then glance again. One of the cobbles is actually a Sonoran mud turtle, an aquatic turtle not much larger than the palm of my hand. Instantly, I want him as much as I wanted that hummingbird nest, or those hapless tadpoles, but I know enough to distrust this yearning. The wanting is the point. If I wait, the wanting will go away. If I wait, the desired object might prove undesirable, or at least neutral, and then I will have to concentrate on wants that cannot be so easily satisfied, the things that do not come in boxes.

Hunkered down on the bottom, the turtle pays no attention to me or to the fish that glide overhead. Sonoran mud turtles eat mostly insects, especially the aquatic larvae of dragonflies, mayflies, and caddisflies, which they catch by lumbering along the bottom, swinging their heads from side to side, lunging at likely tidbits. Given these foraging habits, they aren't likely to catch many fish except as carrion.

This reach of Bear Creek runs through thick oak woods. Here and there the lemonade-berries, a kind of sumac, have turned lemon, copper, and scarlet, dots of color floating against an olive green backdrop. Oak leaves on the ground are saturated with color: gold, tan, sienna, chocolate, ochre. Lizard colors, is how I think of them, and in fact I briefly mistake a fallen leaf for a whiptail lizard. It has the same streamlined shape, the same gold–on–brown venation.

I sit for a moment to listen to the tinkle of water on rock. My friend Ray says that on solo backpacking trips, he sometimes hears human voices in the water. Today, I hear ice cubes being stirred in a tall glass of tea. In myths and fairy tales, running water is respected and revered for its power to give voice to our inmost thoughts and feelings. This is at times a fearful power, a kind of running commentary that might reveal us to others against our will. It is the voice of our guilt, I think, or at least the voice of that constant inner conversation that refuses to be stilled.

The Kaluli of Papua New Guinea turn the music of running water into song. They pattern their music after the pools and drops of mountain streams and feel that composing songs is like having a waterfall in the mind. Your life, the Kaluli say, is a map of where you have lived and traveled, and each song takes a journey into that map. This is an ancient conceit. Perhaps the idea of life as a journey had more resonance long ago when travel was hazardous, its outcome uncertain. Now we travel so frequently that our trips blend into one another, and even the brightest details blur. Journeys are too often repetitive, trivial, perfunctory, exactly what a life should not be.

Hearing Bear Creek sing the song of my life, I respond in kind with the age–old song of water itself. I sing of the time it takes for a drop of rainwater to trickle through gravel and cracks in bedrock before blending into the waters of a surface stream. I sing of the origin of water at the birth of our universe, of its perpetual cycle from earth to sky and back again, never more and never less. I sing of how it shatters into drops, then recombines in silken, sibilant unity. And, like the Kaluli, I sing of how a life, like a stream, is continuous yet never the same. It is a line, a thread, a river, a path, a map.


As Steve and I poke along the stream bottom, hopping every now and then to avoid little pools or patches of wet sand, I feel a moment of pure joy. The sun, warming my face on a chilly day, is part of it. The tiny seeds of grass and sedge, spraying before me as my pant legs brush through the weeds, they are part of it, too, and so are the butterflies and the remnants of summer wildflowers and the lurking turtle and the sycamore leaves swirling downstream.

How, in a world where undiluted joy comes so readily to hand, can anyone claim to be in love with death? The English poet Stevie Smith did. "Sweet Death, kind Death, of all gods you are the best," she wrote. Another time she explained, "I'm nuts on death really, it comes out in my poems and does something to limit their ready sale." Ever the late-season butterfly, I protest. When life holds such sweetness, how can we bear the thought of losing it?

For a moment I regret the months and years when I felt only the burdens of life and none of its joys. In those days, the greater virtue always seemed to lie in being other than I was: brave instead of fearful, beautiful instead of plain, sophisticated instead of ingenuous, talkative instead of quiet, outgoing instead of shy. I was ashamed to be myself, unable to be anyone else. Life was not sweet then. Yet if I had not been so sad in previous years, perhaps I could not be so happy now. We make our lives unnecessarily hard. From long experience, we know what we need to live joyfully: meaningful work, close friendships, loving companionship, meetable challenges, physical activity. So why do we so often fail to achieve the happiness we insist that we desire?

I remember last winter's hike up Ramsey Canyon on the other side of the mountain range. Fresh snow lay six inches deep on fallen logs and stumps. Icicles hung from bedrock ledges. Snowmelt had filled the stream channel, ordinarily dry along its upper reach. Watching the stream tumble and chatter between snowy banks, Steve said, "I hate to see all this water running off. I wish the mountain had some way to absorb and save it for later in the year when it really needs the moisture."

But the mountain can't save its water, nor can we preserve joy against the season of greatest need. The memory of it is as useless as water that has flowed away, as useless as leaves that never fall to the ground. Standing here by Bear Creek, remembering a winter day on the opposite side of the range, I realize that the very sweetness that makes me cling to this place—to life itself—also makes it possible to say, "Yes, now that I have lived it, I can imagine letting it go."

# epilogue

Almost nine months to the day after he submitted his tenure package, Steve called me at work to give me the news. He had gotten tenure. In his hand, he said, was a letter from the dean making it official. I made him read it aloud just so there could be no misunderstanding. He sounded tired and relieved and maybe just the least bit disappointed. Now that he had tenure and his future was mapped out, he could no longer play with the idea that some mysterious destiny awaited him around some unknown corner. Being tenured made it very likely that he would teach and do research at the university until he retired.

Elated and amused and a little bewildered, I observed my own reaction to the good news. For a week, I was so happy that it seemed I would never have cause for unhappiness again. After the delirium subsided, I felt a curious sense of deflation. Yes, it was wonderful to know that his peers valued him and wanted to keep him around. And it was an enormous relief to realize that he would not be unemployed a year from now. But, as much as I had dreaded not knowing where we would be the following year, now that I did know—we would be here, same as always—I almost wished that we were moving on. Had I not spent the past year preparing myself to do just that?

Eventually, of course, I realized that I had also prepared myself to stay. At one point, I dreamed that I was exploring our house. It was oddly unfamiliar, a series of rooms I had never been in, stocked with objects I had never owned. A heady sense of discovery and delight permeated this dream—a sense of enchantment, too. This was supposedly home, by definition the most familiar of familiar places, yet much of it was somehow unknown.

Waking, I remembered that after I wrote a book about the Rincon Mountains east of Tucson, Arizona, many people told me about their experiences there. Everyone who traveled there had a different knowledge of it, and not for the first time I realized how little of that mountain range I really knew. As in my dream, even the places that I might claim to know well are in reality as mysterious to me as the region behind my head.

English essayist Charles Lamb professed himself contented to read the same books, mostly by old-fashioned authors, over and over. Remembering mountains, I understand why. Good mountains, like good books, change as we ourselves change. If I read Shakespeare differently at forty-two than at twenty-two, I inevitably read landscapes differently as well. The best of them reticulate into infinite possibilities, like a river and its hundreds of tributaries, and that is why we can never come to the end of a good mountain.

# notes

## The Gate Swings Wide

A recent history of the Desert Laboratory is Bowers (1990). Biographical sketches of Jacob Blumer and Edith Shreve can be found in Bowers (1983, 1986). Wilson's (1984) readable book of essays is part memoir, part science, part philosophy. Shreve (1917) reported mass emergence of ocotillo in his classic paper on desert seedling establishment. Germination patterns of brittlebush, paloverde, and ocotillo are discussed in Bowers (1994). Bowers and Dimmitt (1994) detail the flowering requirements of brittlebush, ocotillo, and several other desert plants.

## Written on Rock

Schaafsma (1980) presents an authoritative overview of rock art in the American Southwest. For this brief discussion of Hohokam lifeways, I have relied on Gregonis and Reinhard (1979) and Bowden (1977). Bowden reflected on Anglo culture in Dykinga and Bowden (1992). The Wilson quotation is from *Biophilia* (1984). Betancourt and Van Devender (1981) presented the case for human destruction of forests in and around Chaco Canyon.

## A Tango with Bears

The Mary Austin reference is to *Land of Little Rain* (1974). My account of acorn woodpecker ecology is based on Stacey and Koenig (1984) and Mac-Roberts (1970). Brown (1984) reviewed diet of the Arizona gray squirrel. Other animals that depend heavily on acorns are discussed in Pavlik et al. (1991). McPherson (1992) presented data on good years and bad years in oaks. The masting phenomenon in general is reviewed by Silvertown (1980).

## Too Cold for Comfort but Not for Joy

The A. E. Housman quotation is from *A Shropshire Lad*. Both John Jerome quotations are from *The Writing Trade* (1992). Bowers (1980–81) summarized catastrophic freezes in the Sonoran Desert. Steenbergh and Lowe (1977) discussed in great detail the effects of catastrophic frosts on saguaros. Forrest Shreve (1911) showed how freezing temperatures influence saguaro distribution.

## The Brome among the Poppies

Patterns of desert wildflower emergence are described in Juhren et al. (1956) and Beatley (1974). Burgess et al. (1991) discussed introduction of red brome and other exotic annuals to the Sonoran Desert. Tedlock (1992) wrote knowledgeably and empathetically about Zuni culture.

## Unblinkered Eyes

Every visitor to Sabino Canyon should read Lazaroff's (1993) delightful book about its natural and human history. The discussion of hummingbird gorgets is based on Johnsgard (1983).

## Living without Walls

My account of !Kung lifeways relies upon Shostak (1983). Turnbull (1968) and Hudson (1991) gave a sense of how village Africans feel about the bush. Mairs (1990) wrote about wilderness and the human mind. The Bogan quotation is from "Women," the Lizot quotation from *Tales of the Yanomami* (1985). Thoreau wrote about black spruce thickets in *The Maine Woods* (Howarth 1982).

## Encumbered

Annie Dillard's *Pilgrim at Tinker Creek* (1974) is a modern classic. My account of giant water bug life history relies on Smith (1974, 1976).

## Still Hunting

Heinrich (1979) analyzed how bumblebees manage their energy resources. Under the pen name Lewis Carroll, Charles Dodgson (1963) wrote the children's classic referred to in the text. The Joseph Cornell quotation is from *Listening to Nature* (1987).

## A Broken Mountaintop
Sources for this chapter included the original environmental impact assessment for the observatory (USDA Forest Service 1988) and conversations with Paul Young (red squirrels) and Steve McLaughlin (conservation politics). The Gardner quotation is from *On Becoming a Novelist* (1983). Edward Abbey told about pulling surveyors' stakes in *Desert Solitaire* (1968). The Robert Leonard Reid quotation is from his 1991 essay collection.

## From Botanist to Bagworm Lady
The Peg Bracken quotation is from *I Didn't Come Here to Argue* (1954). Stokes's (1983) account of bagworm life history included this quotation.

## High Summer in Heaven
Grant et al. (1990) studied stream–bed morphology in mountainous areas. Stromberg and Patten (1991) reported on the plant ecology of spruce–fir forests in the Pinaleño Mountains.

## Looking into Clear Water
Csikszentmihalyi (1990) said that the human mind can process only seven bits of information at a time. Much of the information in my account of aquatic insect ecology came from Caponigro and Eriksen (1976), Gray (1981), Eriksen et al. (1984), and Cummins and Merritt (1984). The reference to Henry James is from *The Art of the Novel* (1888).

## Gifts Given and Received
Nuñez Cabeza de Vaca (1983) described starving Indian tribes in the American Southwest.

## Walking through Memory
Proudman's (1977) is the indispensable guide to trail building from which much of this information was taken. The Casey quotation is from his book on memory (1987).

## Writing the Future
Our flora of the Huachuca Mountains (Bowers and McLaughlin 1996) describes in greater detail the additions to and subtractions from our preliminary list of plants. Davidson and Rugge's axiom is from their book on canoeing in the wilderness (1983). Charlotte Goodding Reeder told me about her

father, Leslie Goodding. The excerpts from John Bigelow's journal were published in 1968.

## Water Music

Bock and Bock (1985) and Glinski (1977) discussed sycamore reproduction. My account of leaf decomposition in streams is based on Petersen and Cummins (1974). Feld's (1982) account of Kaluli song and poetry makes fascinating reading. The Stevie Smith quotations are borrowed from Cross (1984).

# bibliography

Abbey, E. 1968. *Desert Solitaire: A Season in the Wilderness.* McGraw-Hill, New York.

Austin, M. 1974. *The Land of Little Rain.* University of New Mexico Press, Albuquerque.

Baranski, M. J. 1975. An analysis of variation within white oak (*Quercus alba* L.). *North Carolina Agricultural Experiment Station Technical Bulletin No. 236.*

Beatley, J. C. 1974. Phenological events and their environmental triggers in Mojave Desert ecosystems. *Ecology* 55:856–63.

Betancourt, J. L., and T. R. Van Devender. 1981. Holocene vegetation in Chaco Canyon, New Mexico. *Science* 214:656–58.

Bigelow, J. 1968. *On the Bloody Trail of Geronimo.* Westernlore Press, Los Angeles.

Bock, J. H., and C. E. Bock. 1985. Patterns of reproduction in Wright's sycamore. *USDA Forest Service General Technical Report RM-20.*

Bowden, C. 1977. *Killing the Hidden Waters.* University of Texas Press, Austin.

Bowers, J. E. 1980–81. Catastrophic freezes in the Sonoran Desert. *Desert Plants* 2:232–36.

———. 1983. Jacob Corwin Blumer, Arizona botanist. *Brittonia* 35:197–203.

———. 1986. A career of her own: Edith Shreve at the Desert Laboratory. *Desert Plants* 8:23–29.

———. 1990. A debt to the future: Scientific achievements of the Desert Laboratory, Tumamoc Hill, Tucson, Arizona. *Desert Plants* 10:9–12, 35–47.

———. 1994. Natural conditions for seedling emergence of three woody plants in the northern Sonoran Desert. *Madroño* 41:73–84.

Bowers, J. E., and M. A. Dimmitt. 1994. Flowering phenology of six woody plants in the northern Sonoran Desert. *Bulletin of the Torrey Botanical Club* 121:215–29.

Bowers, J. E., and S. P. McLaughlin. 1996. Flora of the Huachuca Mountains, a botanically rich and historically significant sky island in Cochise County, Arizona. *Journal of the Arizona-Nevada Academy of Science* 29:66–107.

Bracken, P. 1954. *I Didn't Come Here to Argue.* Harcourt Brace Jovanovich, New York.

Brown, D. E. 1984. *Arizona's Tree Squirrels.* Arizona Game and Fish Department, Phoenix.

Burgess, T. L., J. E. Bowers, and R. M. Turner. 1991. Exotic plants at the Desert Laboratory, Tucson, Arizona. *Madroño* 38:96–114.

Caponigro, M. A., and C. H. Eriksen. 1976. Surface film locomotion by the water strider *Gerris remigis. American Midland Naturalist* 95:268–78.

Casey, E. S. 1987. *Remembering: A Phenomenological Study.* Indiana University Press, Bloomington.

Cornell, J. 1987. *Listening to Nature: How to Deepen Your Awareness of Nature.* Dawn Publications, Nevada City, CA.

Cross, A. 1984. *Sweet Death, Kind Death.* Ballantine Books, New York.

Csikszentmihalyi, M. 1990. *Flow: The Psychology of Optimal Experience.* Harper-Collins, New York.

Cummins, K. W., and R. W. Merritt. 1984. Ecology and distribution of aquatic insects. In R. W. Merritt and K. W. Cummins, eds., *An Introduction to the Aquatic Insects of North America,* 2d ed., p. 59–65. Kendall/Hunt, Dubuque, IA.

Davidson, J. W., and J. Rugge. 1983. *The Complete Wilderness Paddler.* Random House, New York.

Dillard, A. 1974. *Pilgrim at Tinker Creek.* Harper's Magazine Press, New York.

Dodgson, C. L. 1963 [1872]. *Through the Looking Glass and What Alice Found There.* Macmillan, New York.

Dykinga, J., and C. Bowden. 1992. *The Sonoran Desert.* Harry N. Abrams, New York.

Eriksen, C. H., V. H. Resh, S. S. Balling, and G. A. Lamberti. 1984. Aquatic insect respiration. In R. W. Merritt and K. W. Cummins, eds., *An Introduction to the Aquatic Insects of North America,* 2d ed., p. 27–37. Kendall/Hunt, Dubuque, IA.

Feld, S. 1982. *Sound and Sentiment: Birds, Weeping, Poetics, and Song in Kaluli Expression.* University of Pennsylvania Press, Philadelphia.

Gardner, J. 1983. *On Becoming a Novelist.* Harper and Row, New York.

Glinski, R. L. 1977. Regeneration and distribution of sycamore and cottonwood trees along Sonoita Creek, Santa Cruz County, Arizona. In R. R.
Johnson and D. A. Jones, technical coordinators, *Importance, Preservation
and Management of Riparian Habitat: A Symposium*, p. 116–23. *USDA Forest
Service General Technical Report RM-43*.

Grant, G. E., F. J. Swanson, and M. Wolman. 1990. Pattern and origin of stepped
bed morphology in high-gradient streams, Western Cascades, Oregon.
*Geological Society of America Bulletin* 102:340–52.

Gray, L. J. 1981. Species composition and life histories of aquatic insects in a
lowland Sonoran Desert stream. *American Midland Naturalist* 106:229–42.

Gregonis, L. M., and K. J. Reinhard. 1979. *Hohokam Indians of the Tucson Basin*.
University of Arizona Press, Tucson.

Heinrich, B. 1979. *Bumblebee Economics*. Harvard University Press, Cambridge, MA.

Howarth, W. 1982. *Thoreau in the Mountains*. Farrar Straus Giroux, New York.

Hudson, M. 1991. *Our Grandmother's Drums*. Henry Holt, New York.

James, H. 1934. *The Art of the Novel*. Scribners, New York.

———. 1979. *Italian Hours*. Grove Press, New York.

Jerome, J. 1992. *The Writing Trade: A Year in the Life*. Viking, New York.

Johnsgard, P. A. 1983. *The Hummingbirds of North America*. Smithsonian Institu-
tion Press, Washington, DC.

Juhren, M., F. W. Went, and E. Phillips. Ecology of desert plants. IV. Combined
field and laboratory work on germination of annuals in the Joshua Tree
National Monument. *Ecology* 37:318–30.

Lazaroff, D. W. 1993. *Sabino Canyon: The Life of a Southwestern Oasis*. University of
Arizona Press, Tucson.

Lizot, J. 1985. *Tales of the Yanomami: Daily Life in the Venezuelan Rain Forest*. Cambridge University Press, New York.

McPherson, G. R. 1992. Ecology of oak woodlands in Arizona. In P. F. Ffolliott
et al. (technical editors), *Symposium on Ecology and Management of Oak and
Associated Woodlands: Perspectives in the Southwestern United States and Northern
Mexico*, p. 24–33. *USDA Forest Service General Technical Report RM-218*.

MacRoberts, M. H. 1970. Notes on the food habits and food defense of the
acorn woodpecker. *Condor* 72:196–204.

Mairs, N. 1990. *Carnal Acts*. HarperCollins, New York.

Nuñez Cabeza de Vaca, Alvar. 1983 [1542, 1555]. *Adventures in the Unknown Interior of America*. Translated and edited by C. Covey. University of New
Mexico Press, Albuquerque.

Pavlik, B. M., P. C. Muick, S. Johnson, and M. Popper. *Oaks of California*. Ca-
chuma Press, Santa Barbara, CA.

Petersen, R. C., and K. W. Cummins. 1974. Leaf processing in a woodland stream ecosystem. *Freshwater Biology* 4:343–68.

Proudman, R. D. 1977. *The AMC Field Guide to Trail Building and Maintenance*. Appalachian Mountain Club.

Reid, R. L. 1991. *Mountains of the Great Blue Dream*. North Point Press, San Francisco.

Schaafsma, P. 1980. *Indian Rock Art of the Southwest*. School of American Research, Santa Fe, NM; University of New Mexico Press, Albuquerque.

Shostak, M. 1983. *Nisa: The Life and Words of a !Kung Woman*. Random House, New York.

Shreve, F. 1911. The influence of low temperatures on the distribution of the giant cactus. *Plant World* 14:136–46.

———. 1917. The establishment of desert perennials. *Journal of Ecology* 5:210–16.

Silvertown, J. W. 1980. The evolutionary ecology of mast seeding in trees. *Biological Journal of the Linnean Society* 14:235–50.

Smith, R. L. 1974. Life history of *Abedus herberti* in central Arizona (Hemiptera: Belostomatidae). *Psyche* 81:272–83.

———. 1976. Male brooding behavior of the water bug *Abedus herberti* (Hemiptera: Belostomatidae). *Annals of the Entomological Society of America* 69:740–47.

Stacey, P. B., and W. D. Koenig. 1984. Cooperative breeding in the acorn woodpecker. *Scientific American* (August):114–21.

Steenbergh, W. F., and C. H. Lowe. 1977. *Ecology of the Saguaro: II. Reproduction, Germination, Establishment, Growth, and Survival of the Young Plant*. National Park Service Scientific Monograph Series No. 8. GPO, Washington, DC.

Stokes, D. W. 1983. *A Guide to Observing Insect Lives*. Little, Brown, Boston.

Stromberg, J. C., and D. T. Patten. 1991. Dynamics of the spruce–fir forests on the Pinaleño Mountains, Graham County, Arizona. *Southwestern Naturalist* 36:37–48.

Tedlock, B. 1992. *The Beautiful and the Dangerous: Encounters with the Zuni Indians*. Viking, New York.

Turnbull, C. M. 1968. *The Forest People*. Simon and Schuster, New York.

USDA Forest Service. 1988. Final environmental impact statement, proposed Mt. Graham Astrophysical Area, Pinaleño Mountains, Coronado National Forest. Coronado National Forest, Tucson, AZ.

Wilson, E. O. 1984. *Biophilia: The Human Bond with Other Species*. Harvard University Press, Cambridge, MA.

# about the author

Janice Emily Bowers is the author of *A Full Life in a Small Pla[...] Mountains Next Door*, and other books about the natural world. F[...] past sixteen years, she has worked as a botanist for the U.S. Geol[...] Survey. She lives on the outskirts of Tucson with her husband [...] McLaughlin, her cat, Katie, and a red-spotted toad, Little Budd[...]